Growth Without Inequality

Many years on after the 2007–8 financial crisis, most developed nations still find themselves in a state of weak recovery, high debt pile-up and distributive disparity. The intriguing question that we face is whether the golden days of modern capitalism are over, or if capitalism is just undergoing another period of adjustment characteristic of its past. What is disheartening is that the twin economic goals of sustainable growth and equality, which the world has now come to recognise as of paramount importance but mutually conflicting, remain, more now than ever, illusive and unattainable.

Growth Without Inequality attempts to address this issue and to provide a pragmatic solution especially for nations in the current policy gridlock. By offering a unified framework of factors that drive growth, it shows how growth also gives rise to an array of "anomalous market forms" (defined by different degrees of value and risk visibility) that subvert distributive equity between labour and capital. It debunks both the pure free market solution and the mixed economy approach on the ground that they fail to arrest the growth-propelling yet subversive power inherent in the "corporate forms" under the present capitalistic regime.

Having shown that effective reform can hardly take place within the system itself, this book proposes to build a separate sector (Economy II) and partition it from the existing system (Economy I). The solution is easy to implement and quick to take effect. By one single stroke, this "Non-Marxist" solution can happily achieve the ideals of both "competitive capitalism" and "egalitarian socialism".

Henry K. H. Woo is an economic methodologist. He is the founder of the International Network for Economic Method and the Founding Chairman of the Hong Kong Institute of Economic Science. Apart from researches on economic theory and methodology, he also publishes widely on cultural studies, China's economy, political and educational issues.

Banking, Money and International Finance

For a full list of titles in this series, please visit www.routledge.com/series/BMIF

Growth Without Inequality
Reinventing Capitalism

Henry K. H. Woo

Routledge
Taylor & Francis Group

LONDON AND NEW YORK

First published 2017
by Routledge

2 Park Square, Milton Park, Abingdon, Oxfordshire OX14 4RN
52 Vanderbilt Avenue, New York, NY 10017

Routledge is an imprint of the Taylor & Francis Group, an informa business

First issued in paperback 2019

British Library Cataloguing-in-Publication Data
A catalogue record for this book is available from the British Library

Library of Congress Cataloging-in-Publication Data
Names: Hu, Guoheng, author.
Title: Growth without inequality : reinventing capitalism /
Henry K.H. Woo.
Description: Abingdon, Oxon ; New York, NY : Routledge, 2017. |
Includes index.
Identifiers: LCCN 2016044684 | ISBN 9780415793209 (hardback) |
ISBN 9781315211213 (ebook)
Subjects: LCSH: Economic development. | Capitalism. | Equality.
Classification: LCC HD82 .H775 2017 | DDC 338.9--dc23
LC record available at https://lccn.loc.gov/2016044684

ISBN: 978-0-415-79320-9 (hbk)
ISBN: 978-0-367-88696-7 (pbk)

Typeset in Times New Roman
by Taylor & Francis Books

Contents

Preface

I write this book with three goals in mind. First and foremost, I hope to offer a lasting solution to the major malaises of present-day capitalism, a solution that is at once feasible and simple to implement. This is the most important goal because it can affect directly the welfare of most people, especially the less privileged. Second, I wish to give a novel diagnosis on the merits and failings of capitalism, on how capitalism first brings prosperity to the modern world and then how capitalism, as it matures, gives rise to so many difficulties that haunt our time. Needless to say, the usefulness of the solution I offer is independent of the correctness of my diagnosis, for a solution can still be correct and functional for the wrong reason. Third, as a corollary of my diagnosis, I wish to present a new economic paradigm, which I believe stands some chance of revolutionising our economic thinking and of liberating us from the dead-weight of the drawbacks of modern economics which has, sad to say, lost its bearing even as it evolves into a highly sophisticated discipline.

Conventional wisdom has it that the evolution of economic thought closely follows the nature of the imperative economic question posed of the day, which inevitably reflects the problems of the time. While this may well be the case, this also indicates that economics is still a developing science, for a truly mature science should have encompassed and anticipated most of the likely scenarios. In the founding days of modern economics, i.e. in the days of classical economics when industrialisation began to take place, the principal question asked was whether or not and in what way economic growth is possible. As more formal, analytical tools developed, the question gradually shifted to one of efficiency, i.e. how resources can be allocated efficiently at the level of the firm and the individual. A corollary question was why and how a competitive, self-equilibrating market can result in the highest level of welfare for all. As the world was politically split into polarised ideological camps, the question asked was what kind of economic system promises a higher level of performance and distributive justice. The subsequent harsh experiences of the Great Depression forced economists to focus their principal question on macro-stability, namely, what factors lead to the instability of an economy and what tools we can rely upon to address the problem. Even as the Great Depression is far behind us, the shadow it casts and the Great Recession that we recently experience once again inspire economists of our time to reformulate the way we think about problems arising from both the monetary and the real sides of the economy, for example unemployment, debt, macro-stability and the role of government in managing an economy.

As Third World nations awakened to the need to develop their economies in the post-World War II era, the question of growth and development, although a side show, began to draw considerable attention. In the recent decade, as economists and lay people alike become keenly aware of the growing disparity between the rich and the poor, a strong demand for redistribution is building up around the world. Robert Schiller goes so far as saying that rising inequality is the most important economic problem of the day. The question of how an economy should redistribute income has now come to front stage. But no satisfactory answer has been offered up to date.

Notwithstanding the vicissitudes of these questions and their respective research focuses in different periods of economic theorising, the single most important economic question that should be asked, in the ultimate analysis and across all ages, is whether or not and how an economy is able to achieve reasonable growth and equality (in the broad sense) simultaneously. This issue is of paramount and profound importance because once these twin goals can be concurrently achieved, the problems of micro-efficiency, macro-stability, or of development, can by default be solved, for it is quite inconceivable that an economy that keeps growing and that takes good care of its less privileged can be inefficient and unstable. Even if the latter problems were to stay, they may be transitory and of a lesser magnitude.

Scholars, especially those on the left wing or on the doomsday front, are very much inclined to raise big and eye-ball catching questions about the economic future of humankind. One familiar and recurrent theme is the fate of capitalism in general and whether capitalism can overcome its inherent failings in particular.

Optimists argue that capitalism by virtue of its openness, its self-regulating, self-correcting and self-perfecting capability, is always moving onto a more mature plane, in spite of its inevitable but occasional setbacks. Since the ability of mankind to learn from his experiences is without bound, capitalism, despite its vagaries, will, given time, transform itself into a system most suited to human nature and to the needs of human livelihood.

Pessimists, however, think otherwise. They believe that the inherent failings of capitalism are not going to be healed. What we are now witnessing is probably the beginning of the last phase of capitalism, namely, a stalemate characterised by low or nil growth caused by the changing nature of technology and increasing maldistribution with dire socio-political consequences. Most of us moderate scholars, averse to making bold and sweeping generalisations, would prefer not to treat the ills of capitalism on a categorical basis and prefer to look at its ills individually.

Generally speaking, economists holding the middle ground of this theoretical spectrum choose to identify and address some most disturbing trends about present-day capitalism which become particularly conspicuous after the 2007–8 financial crash. One is macro-instability. The question is whether or not the financial sector with its propensity to accommodate speculative activities, but which is considered part and parcel of modern capitalism, can be tamed. Another question is how the growing public debt and its negative impacts can be properly managed. A further trend which causes concern is that there are signs that, as the "low-hanging fruits" are plucked (Cowen), technological progress may slow down, thus dampening one of the most important driving forces behind growth. And probably the most disturbing trend of all is distributive disparity and its related problems of high rates of unemployment and wage rate stagnation, which seem to worsen with each passing decade.

As the above trends converge, partisan struggle and ideological conflicts will intensify, leading to hard-to-govern situations and even dysfunctional governments and failing states, especially as national debts soar in many nations and as servicing costs threaten to go up. Briefly put, modern capitalism as we witness in today's developed world is now in a double predicament, i.e., slower growth with rising inequality. Looking ahead, modern capitalism, trapped in the vicious circle of rising inequality threatening to slow down growth and slower growth in turn aggravating inequality, seems to be sliding into the worst of the possible worlds. And sad to say, no solution is in sight. No wonder pessimists raise time and again the question whether capitalism has run its course or at least, whether or not the peak of capitalism is already behind us.

The analysis I make in this book agrees that modern capitalism is in real trouble, but this is largely the result of its own doing. It is true that the institutions that characterise capitalism are highly conducive to growth, but as I have taken pains to demonstrate, economic growth, by empowering the moneyed class and their corporations politically and economically and in giving rise to a high-return seeking financial sector that accommodates the activities of these corporations as well as the surplus wealth they accumulate or inherit, eventually subverts its own goal. Capitalism, having undergone phases of wealth creation through mass participation and with relatively acceptable levels of distributive equity, crawls insidiously back to a game largely dominated by the rich, the elite and their "accomplices". The result is mounting maldistribution, social tension and political disarray, the kind of threats outlined in the above paragraph.

These malaises, in my opinion, are not the inherent properties of capitalism as an institution in the broad sense. They are instead the result of the working of several key operating mechanisms or micro-features of capitalism that unwittingly gives undue power to the rich or capital (as opposed to labour). These include, among others, the unbounded scalability of the limited liability joint stock company and its highly asymmetric risk-return but growth-propelling characteristic, the predatory behaviour of the holding company that matches perfectly the appetite of financiers, the asymmetry of credit access between the poor and the rich, the tolerance of growing leverage and excessive speculation in the modern financial system with its wealth-destroying cycles. As long as these institutional mechanisms are in place, maldistribution is unstoppable and the vicious circle goes on. The paradox is that the engines that once bring about growth and prosperity turn out to be the same ones that cause the economic malaises we face today.

The solution to these malaises, however, is not to radically change these basic institutional designs or "genes". Dropping these mechanisms can be likened to pouring the baby out with the bathwater. For all their drawbacks, they contribute significantly to the spectacular performance of the modern economy. Drastic changes of these mechanisms are also too radical because the results are not easily unpredictable. Repairs to obvious excesses are necessary but wholesale changes are too dangerous to contemplate. But on the other hand, minor and marginal modifications of the system are unlikely to produce strong and desirable effects.

The solution offered in this book is to create a dual economy in the true sense. I propose to split the overall economy into two parts, namely Economy I and Economy II. Economy I represents the continuation of the present capitalist system without any big change (except making repairs and amendments to its major defects which I will not deal with in this book). Economy II, on the other hand, is a new construct built from square one under a scheme that I name the NPV (Natural Person-Voucher) scheme. Economy II is going have a simple mode of operation to be characterised by the self-equilibrating market form and corporate entities in the most primitive form. The participants are limited to natural persons (as opposed to legal or more precisely, juridical persons) and the initial funding is to be provided by the government in the form of vouchers. Economy II is to be partitioned from Economy I and is designed to be insulated from the adverse impacts of the latter. Financial resources from Economy I in the form of loans are in principle permitted to flow into Economy II, but active participants in Economy I are barred from participating and holding shares in Economy II. Participants in Economy II are restricted to operate only by "natural person companies" and "natural partnership companies". They are to be formed legally by natural persons, who are restricted from holding shares in any other natural personal companies (although they may hold shares of companies in Economy I as sleeping shareholders).

The purchasing power of Economy II is injected by the government in the form of general purpose and specific purpose vouchers. The idea is to induce low skilled and less resourceful individuals who are not in a position to compete in Economy I to contribute to and participate in Economy II characterised by a far more level playing field. With purchasing power steadily and carefully injected into Economy II, business opportunities and competitive markets gradually open up, with the higher performing individuals standing to gain while the underperformers are still able to earn a decent living on their own effort through the trickle down effect. On the supply side, since resources in Economy I are allowed to flow into Economy II either in the form of loan[1] or in the form of existing, qualified firms applying to change to the status of natural person company, it is expected that over time Economy II will grow with the aid of these resources on top of government spending and re-cycled earnings within Economy II.

Over time, with human capital formation steadily taking place among the initially less skilled group, and with Economy II generally specialising in labour-intensive and service-intensive sectors, we can expect a macro division of labour to eventually emerge, with Economy I specialising in industries requiring sophisticated management, complex organisation, cutting-edge technology, highly professional people and big capital investment, while Economy II specialises in labour-intensive and service-intensive sectors requiring less knowledge, management, capital and technology input. Economy II, being sealed off from the negative impacts of Economy I and its cyclical fluctuations, can be expected to grow steadily with the accumulation of human capital.

On the ramifications of Economy II, I will devote an entire chapter (Chapter 5) to explaining its merits, notably how it contributes to equality, growth, macro-stability, individual well-being and social harmony. It is, of course, not easy to predict how large and powerful an Economy II in any particular nation will eventually become and to what extent it might significantly supplement its Economy I, because that would depend on the level and rate of voucher injection (i.e. the long-term funding position) and the responsiveness of its participants, among other factors.

In the wake of the 2007–8 financial crash, many solutions, both short-term and long-term, have been offered to repair the shortcomings that are supposed to cause the instability of the capitalist system as well as its other weaknesses. Some commonly raised solutions include reforming the financial sector for greater stability, putting in more investment in education and public infrastructure to maintain long-term productivity, promoting corporate social responsibility to arrest the widening distributive gap, among others. While these solutions may bring about some stability and growth to the economy, it is difficult to see how they can effectively address the core problem, namely, to sustain reasonable growth without deteriorating maldistribution, bearing in mind the fact that economic growth will persistently aggravate the imbalance of economic power between capital and labour. Even granted that these solutions can solve part of the problem, they would need time to take effect. My proposed NPV scheme, on the other hand, has the double merit of being easy to implement and quicker to yield positive results.

For any solution to a problem to be effective, it ought to be simple and easy to implement. As far as possible, it should also try to avoid disrupting the status quo. Together, these attributes constitute what I call the "principle of minimalism", which is important to the success of any public policy measure. Otherwise, it may meet with resistance from the establishment or the invested interests and may generate uncertainties that erode the confidence of the participants in question. My proposal of building a brand-new Economy II under the NPV scheme has exactly this merit, because it will neither directly challenge the interests of the establishment nor confront the existing interest groups.

Moreover, a prosperous Economy II can be expected to inject life and vitality into Economy I beyond the short term.

All in all, the NPV scheme I propose in this book should in principle achieve the twin ideals of both "egalitarian socialism" and "competitive capitalism". Under this scheme, the two ideals are neither mutually exclusive nor are simple trade-offs. This world of ours is not going to be a perfect one, because all individuals are born with different endowments, material or genetic. Social arrangements should in essence be such that the inequalities thus generated be minimised or at least rendered innocuous. But then there is a paradox. If the social arrangement is so designed that there is too little inequality in material outcome, there would remain hardly any incentive to drive the high-performers to a new plane of achievement. For optimality, social arrangements should be so organised as to accommodate both the high-achievers and the not-so-high ones, to reward the former as far as possible in order to retain the driving force of an economy, but also to unleash whatever potentials there are in the not-so-high achievers. Only by partitioning the overall economy in the way I propose in this book can we come near to such an ideal arrangement.

In my mind, the NPV scheme I propose is particularly suited to the conditions of China. In the first instance, it fits well with the professed vision of the present political regime which claims to be adhering to a special form of socialism (specifically called Chinese-style socialism), in spite of its vigorous adoption of the market mechanism in the post-Mao era. Painfully aware of the disastrous consequences brought about by the kind of blanket egalitarianism under the Mao regime, Deng Xiaoping adopts the market approach to unleash individual incentive, in open admission that this would bring about income and wealth inequality in the first phase of implementation. This dose of medicine works well. China miraculously moves onto the path of prosperity. But the price to pay is deteriorating economic inequality. If the problem is not addressed in time, the rising inequality will pose an obstacle to further growth in a way quite similar to what the Western world is experiencing. In the years to come, the situation will further deteriorate with a fast ageing population, partly as a result of its one-child policy.[2] The timely erection of Economy II can come to soothe this potential problem.

Moreover, a prosperous Economy II is particularly suited to China because it then no longer has to depend heavily on cutting-edge technological progress for economic growth, which it commands with relatively less advantage at this stage of development. Besides, China's sizeable population means that a higher unemployment rate may have a serious consequence on its socio-political stability. Economy II, which targets at creating mass employment among the less privileged, is well suited to preventing such adverse development.

The erection of Economy II depends on and implies the incubation of different types of new markets through the issue of "supply-side" vouchers geared to both the labour endowment of an economy as well as the aspirations of its lower-level skilled workers. As such, the market mechanism is central to the working of Economy II, as much as it is indispensable to the operation of Economy I.

However, as this book shows, in spite of the instrumentality of the market in achieving efficiency, the fact remains that changing corporate forms both in the real sector and the financial sector can give rise to less-than-efficient or even highly risky markets, and that economic growth through these new market forms can lead to serious maldistribution in the longer run. Considering these points together, my view of the market is that, in spite of its indispensability, it is at best a neutral platform (depending on the type of "market form" it takes), but one that is incapable of solving economic ills across the board. At the worst, market operation under some less efficient "market forms" may lead to serious mispricings of values and risks and can thus be a problem creator rather than a problem solver. Recall the fact that the market cannot stop the formation and burst of financial bubbles, arrest the ups and downs of economic cycles and achieve a more equitable distribution. Those economists who still believe or insist that the market is a panacea for all malaises should perhaps humbly reflect on such facts instead of just blaming the government for failures that are actually caused by some "anomalous" markets forms brought about by growth-propelling but "subversive" "corporate forms".

This misunderstanding about the nature of the market, in particular its limits, limitations and failures, reflects a deep flaw in modern economics. At the risk of over-generalisation, one can say that modern economics is technically robust and sophisticated, but conceptually weak or even flawed in certain important areas. This is quite ironical, as it gives us the impression that it is already a mature science, in spite of the fact that it cannot explain even the most fundamental phenomena including growth, stability and distribution. One cannot, of course, deny that a lot of economic insights and concepts do throw light on narrowly focused issues and phenomena. However, given the fact that up until today we still do not even have a full grasp of the nature and limitation of the market, which is so central to the study of the economic reality, no wonder we do not have silver bullets for the most burning problems of our time, let alone an answer to keep an economy growing without hurting the interests of people who are less resourceful and less skilled.

In my diagnosis of economic predicaments, I point out that the price signal, being subject to manipulation and influenced by certain institutional mechanisms, is by itself not reliable enough to reflect both real value and risk. Hence it is liable to mislead the economic player who relies solely on it for the formulation of his plans and decisions. Modern economics, eager to do away with the more "slippery" notion of value, also puts undue weight on the price signal and the associate notion of efficiency. This "efficiency paradigm", which constitutes the theoretical foundation of conventional economics, and upon which an elaborate technical edifice has been built, suffers from three basic limitations. First, it is confined largely to understanding at a micro level how the price system works. Second, it focuses narrowly on the prototypic "market form" characterised by a highly competitive goods market with mostly homogeneous products, while ignoring other anomalies. Last but not least, it is fundamentally a static approach, albeit sometimes dressed as a dynamic one.

Alternatively put, mainstream economics adopts a "reductionist approach", trying to explain all economic phenomena by constructing models built solely on measurable variables, in particular prices and price-related variables. This approach, while seemingly scientific, is actually a metaphysical one, using in a reverse manner sophisticated mathematics as a metaphor to explain relatively simple real-life phenomena. Moreover, it has the unfortunate consequence of ignoring the centrality of the more intangible concept of value. It assumes that economic phenomena can be adequately explained without the need to consider the complex and diverse relationships between price and value and their possible gaps which, as I will analyse in this book, constitute and define different "market forms" and by corollary, different types of market failures. In other words, the conventional approach assumes that there is no mispricing of value in the world of exchange. But it is not that mainstream economists who make this apparently simplistic assumption, i.e. values as exchange values, so that prices generally reflect value or in more extreme cases, prices are equatable to or simply equal value, are simple-minded. It is because the earlier masters have spent painstaking effort to look for a single objective bedrock of standard for value, for instance the labour theory of value, in vain. It has taken much intellectual ingenuity, through William Stanley Jevons, Carl Menger, to Leon Walrus, among others, to have finally reconciled the subjective and objective dimensions of value by integrating the notion of scarcity and the associate theory of marginal utility, thus avoiding the daunting if not impossible task of finding a yardstick for the "real" value of everything. Having laid down this theoretical groundwork, it would seem safe to reduce value to the narrow notion of exchange value and by corollary, to price without further ado. This in itself is no mean achievement.

But the price to be paid for by such reductionism is that modern economics, building on prices alone, is dangerously monolithic and lacks the explanatory power it hopes for. This book proposes to remedy this drawback by bringing back the concept of value to the centre stage of economic analysis and proposes to replace the "price paradigm" (or "efficiency paradigm") by the "price–value–risk paradigm". As this book shows, only when we consider a full spectrum of price–value relationships and their corresponding "market forms" can we truly grasp the many economic anomalies of our time, including rent extracting behaviours, deteriorating unemployment, high CEO salary, financial instability and so on.

An arch economic fact of everyday life is that mispricings of value and risk are common, yet not widely recognised. Conventional economic wisdom holds that these are due largely to either market failure or government failure. In this book, I argue that the chief villains (ironically also the same agents that propel growth) are actually the firms that evolve along with economic growth into increasingly complex forms that impact the structure of the markets within which they operate and render them less value-visible and risk-visible. Thus instead of attributing economic problems either to market failure or government failure, we now have a new dimension to consider, i.e. "corporate failure" (in the sense of corporate entities being wittingly and unwittingly able to subvert the "normal" functioning of the market). Indeed, future research is advised to explore into the intricate triangular relationship between government failure, market failure and "corporate failure".

In the course of economic growth in both the real sector and the financial sector, firms continually undergo a process of metamorphosis and take on new "corporate forms". Alongside the more primitive ones of sole proprietorship and partnership with unlimited liability, come the limited liability joint-stock company, the leverage-using bank, the multi-level holding company and more recently, the shadow bank as well as "pass-through corporate structures" targeting to side-step regulation or taxation. The important point to note is that these corporate forms, characterised by increasing complexity and rent-extracting power as well as being congenial to financial manipulation, have become unwittingly the causal propagators of market failures.

I propose to put value back to the centre stage of economics for an additional reason. As I will argue in my analysis of economic growth, the phenomena of growth can be more fruitfully understood by adopting my twin notions of risk ascertainability and value ascertainability, both being essential conditions for growth. I take pains to explain that important economic malaises of our time can also be traced to the lapse of our general ability to ascertain value in relation to the prices transacted. Our diminishing ability to ascertain value relative to price is well exemplified by the rent-seeking and rent-capturing behaviours of the firm. In a similar vein, our diminished ability to ascertain value in relation to risk also leads to highly speculative behaviours in the financial markets, cumulating in bubble and bust. Value in relation to price on one hand and to risk on the other hand thus plays a pivotal role both in economic growth and economic stability. Just as high levels of value and risk visibility create the very conditions for economic growth, it is the very loss of value and risk transparency that leads to financial collapse. If we want an economics that possesses the right kind of academic resources to explain and predict economic behaviours and phenomena, value (in relation to both price and risk) must be restored to its rightful place. Adopting a paradigm based upon the foundational notions of risk and value visibility and ascertainability in relation to price is, therefore, the first step in the building of a new economics. By extension, the new economics should address the typology of "market forms" and "corporate forms" as well as their multi-faceted relationships, in particular their synergetic or subversive relationships. Given that value involves subjective dimensions and is, therefore, less amenable to measurement, we can expect the new economics to be less mathematically rigorous than what we now have under the present price paradigm, but then what we gain is an economics that can explain more.

Fortunately, the solution I propose, although relying heavily on the market, need not worry about the problems faced by Economy I, i.e. growth driven by highly scalable corporate forms leading to the proliferation of multiple, complex "market forms" with varying degrees of value invisibility and their risk ramifications. Since Economy II employs chiefly the most primitive and efficient market form where price more or less reflects value, there is no need for me to first solve the deep philosophical problem of value that haunts our past great masters before making my recommendation.

Finally, a word on the philosophical dimension of the twin notions of risk and value ascertainability. Using these twin notions as an anchor to a new economics amounts philosophically to positing that we accept ignorance as the arch fact of economic life and that the degree of risk and value ascertainability reflects our level of ignorance. The extent of economic progress we make thus reflects how far we succeed in overcoming such ignorance, i.e. in improving the risk and value visibility of both the operating environment as well as our capability to ascertain such risk and value in our actual experiences. By extension, the progress of economics itself also depends on how successfully we manage to decipher and articulate these variables. But alas, instead of starting from the basis of ignorance and working upwards, we have chosen to close our door of understanding by first making metaphysical "perfection assumptions" of information, knowledge, market, rationality, etc. Partly as a result, economics, which is supposed to be a "science of price" narrowly construed, has become a "metaphysics of price". This is, in short, the most fatal flaw of modern economics.

Notes

1 The magnitude of loan may or may not be restricted and the magnitude of restriction should depend on individual circumstances.
2 After thirty years or so of implementation, this policy is recently permitted to be gradually and conditionally relaxed.

Acknowledgements

A number of people have given me support and encouragement in the process of writing, editing and publishing this book and I would like to thank them all.

For typing of the text, information search and collection, as well as general assistance, I would like to extend my thanks to Shaun Lee, Angel Dai, Patricia Woo, Walter Woo, Liu Kin Ming, Canice Ngan, Francis Kwan, Albert Chen, Bill Fang, Stephen Mak, Stephen Cheung Man, K. K. Wong, Sarah Monks, Chris Chan, Jacqueline Chan, Loretta Chen, Vincent Chan, Howard Cheung, Francis T. Lui, Ronald Tam, Sunny Ng, Michelle Leung and Paul Chow.

For their invaluable professional comments and editing work, I am very much indebted to Richard Y. C. Wong, Jim Barth, Rosemary Woo, Jill Yan, Issac Lee, Gerard Chung, David Tang, C. L. Wu and K. K. Fung.

Last but not least, I wish to express my deepest gratitude to all members of the editorial team at Routledge, especially Kristina Abbotts, Elanor Best, Cathy Hurren and Liz Nichols, who have been most helpful throughout the process of publishing the work.

Part I
Diagnosis

1 Growth and Its Drivers

1.1 A Critique of the Standard Growth Theory

The Deficiency of the Neo-Classical Growth Theory

I take the standard growth theory to consist broadly of the neo-classical growth theory and its descendants, including those competing growth theories that attempt to make up for the former's weakness. The neo-classical growth theory itself takes as its point of departure the aggregate production function, a concept borrowed from the production function at the level of the firm.

Assuming away population growth as well as technological progress, the only remaining growth driver for the neo-classical growth theory is capital accumulation, which is taken to be a function of the level of savings. But by assuming diminishing marginal productivity, national income will not grow as fast as the capital stock. As a result, savings will not grow as fast as depreciation. Eventually, depreciation will catch up with savings. At this point, the capital stock will stop rising and growth in national income will come to an end. That is to say, any attempt to boost growth by encouraging people to save more will ultimately fail.

But here we face an empirical problem. Since we observe sustained long-run growth in output per person in advanced countries since the Industrial Revolution, there must have existed something that offsets the law of diminishing marginal productivity. By the logic of common sense, the neo-classical growth theorist infers that this something must be technological progress. In his scheme of things, technological progress is brought about by some unspecified process that generates scientific discovery and technological diffusion. And by implication, growth is driven and sustained by technological progress in the long run. Some stronger version even posits that the rate of growth is determined by the rate of technological progress (Harrod, 1939).

Since the aggregate production function itself does not provide a place for technological progress as a core factor of production, the ingenious (and face-saving) repair work that the neo-classical growth theorist does is to assign it the status of an exogenous factor (of production), an allegedly important input but one which is outside the regular production system.

The *"Endogenisation Project"*

But common sense also tells us that technological progress is not entirely a factor outside the production system, for there are good reasons to believe that technological progress also depends on economic decisions within the production system. To resolve the problem, the more enlightened growth theorist makes an attempt to bring technological progress into the system itself, under the high-sounding banner of "endogenisation".

Arrow (1962), for example, argues that technological progress takes place in the process of producing capital goods because people learn by doing. That is, when people and firms accumulate capital, their learning process engenders knowledge externalities and thereby technological progress as an unintended consequence. This results in raising the marginal productivity of capital, thus offsetting the tendency for marginal productivity to diminish when technology remains unchanged. This set of hypothesis, also known as the AK theory, posits new and positive links between physical capital and human capital (e.g. Lucas, 1988).

The AK model, representing an earlier version of the "endogenisation" effort, is only half-baked, for it does not make an explicit distinction between capital accumulation and technological progress. According to the AK paradigm, knowledge accumulation leading to technological breakthrough is a serendipitous by-product of capital accumulation. Thrift, efficiency of resources allocation and capital accumulation still occupy centre stage in driving the long-run growth of an economy. The best way to sustain high growth rates is to save a large fraction of GDP, some of which will find its way into financing a higher rate of technological progress, thus resulting in faster growth.

Second-wave and more fully-fledged "endogenised" growth theories include innovation-based growth models (e.g. Romer's product-variety model (1990)), according to which, innovation causes productivity growth by creating new varieties of products. Another branch, also known as Schumpeterian growth theory, developed by Aghion and Howitt (1992), focuses on quality-improving innovations that render old products obsolete. The latter enjoys the advantage of presenting an explicit analysis of the innovation process underlying long-run growth.

All in all, the "endogenisation project" consists of two key features. First, it emphasises the more qualitative dimensions of growth and second, it espouses the operating principle of increasing returns.

Interestingly, and as may well be expected, the debate between the original neo-classical growth theory and its descendent AK theories which focus more on capital accumulation, i.e. the quantitative aspects of growth, as well as the competing product varieties and Schumpeterian school, which emphasise innovation that raises productivity, focuses logically on how much growth is attributable to the accumulation of physical and human capital and how much to innovation and technological progress.

Interpreting the "Solow Residual"

To answer this question, growth economists devised an indigenous method to ascertain the relative contributions of different factors to economic growth under the term "growth accounting" (Solow, 1957). The surprising result from the many studies using this method is that a sizeable portion of national growth fails to be accounted for by the growth of the capital stock and the growth of the workforce. The residual which is commonly called the "Solow residual", is what is left after netting out the effects of labour and capital (i.e. the portion of growth that cannot be explained by these quantifiable factors[1]). A study shows that as much as two-thirds of the growth rate in the OECD countries goes unexplained (Aghion and Howitt, 2009).

The magnitude of the residual takes growth economists by surprise. There are generally three lines of responses. The most direct one is to assume that the residual, or the "magic factor", is identical with technological progress, thus logically extending the widely received and common-sense view of taking technological progress as the driver of growth.

To the more cautious economists, interpreting the residual as "total factor productivity" (TFP) (which focuses on how an economy uses its factors of production productively or in short, as a "catch all" factor) seems more appropriate. For poorer nations, since they have a small capital stock per capita, a high savings rate would substantially increase investment and growth. But for rich and mature nations, which have already a large capital stock, how productively an economy uses it matters a lot. In this interpretation, "total factor productivity", despite the vagueness and almost mythical connotation of the notion, is taken to be the principal contributor of economic growth. Curiously enough, although it remains methodologically a semi-finished and a half-way-house concept, it has been complacently assumed to be a fully fledged causal growth factor. The advantage of taking this semi-finished concept as a final explanatory variable is, of course, that there is no further need to make causal enquiry into other engines of growth.

There are sceptics who are not prepared to commit to any position. The "magic factor", as Abramovitz (1993) famously puts it, is in effect a "measure of our ignorance". But alas, the residual is too big to be ignored. And the ignorance is simply unforgivable.

Perhaps being too pre-occupied with identifying the residual with technological progress which itself is a causal factor, the above interpretations including that of total factor productivity fall under the category which I would call the "causal factor interpretation". That is, instead of first enquiring into the very nature of the residual as revealed in the growth accounting studies, the economists concerned jump the gun to enquire into the causal factors that account for the residual. This is not a bad idea, because at one stage or another, we have to seek causal explanations. But before that, it is perhaps more appropriate to find out, from the accounting point of view, what that residual actually consists of in the first place. This approach I would call "the factor receipt" or "factor payment" approach.

The difficulty with the technological progress explanation or any other causal factor explanation is that these causal factors must have been significantly if not already fully reflected in the factor payments already received by both labour and capital. For it is simply inconceivable that labour and capital receive payments for their contribution independent of the knowledge or the technology they respectively embody. The market prices upon which the growth accounting statistics are compiled must have fully reflected the currently applied knowledge and technology respectively embodied in labour and capital. For otherwise, such labour and capital would fail to stay competitive in the market. Simply put, when aggregate output rises, is it either because we have employed more capital goods or because we have employed better ones? The truth is, of course, both. Hence the Solow residual can hardly reflect some disembodied technologies or some vague and mythical factors over and above the technologies currently in use. Disembodied technology is, in short, incompatible with growth accounting statistics. The same argument also applies to labour.

If the causal factor approach is not a viable line of enquiry, a sensible option is to return to the more fundamental question, i.e., what is the nature of the residual as a factor receipt. Bluntly put, who gets this residual receipt? On this, I will revert in a later chapter.

The Flaws of the Standard Growth Theory

That the standard growth theory, in particular the neo-classical growth theory, is flawed, is beyond dispute. The interesting question though, is how the flaw comes about. There are two dimensions to this analysis, namely, the methodological dimension and the metaphysical dimension.

The neoclassical growth theory takes as its point of departure the neo-classical aggregate production function, where output is assumed to be governed by labour and capital stock as well as the operating assumption of diminishing marginal productivity. This point of departure, borrowed straightforwardly from the product function at the level of the firm, is merely an expedient. The neo-classical growth theorist has apparently not given sufficiently careful consideration to whether or not the "wholesale" transplantation is legitimate or appropriate. For it is quite obvious that the aggregate production function at the level of the economy can hardly match, in almost every respect, the production function at the level of the firm. The latter is chiefly of an engineering nature, whereas the former is more of a managerial one, hence more plastic and sensitive to a wide array of external influences. Thus from the very beginning, the neo-classical growth theory focusing exclusively on labour and capital as its core variables is too narrowly based. Moreover, the amenability of these two core variables to easy measurement renders the theory susceptible to quantitative bias, ignoring unwittingly qualitative factors that may have a role to play in economic growth.

The consequence of the narrow focus reinforced by a quantitative bias is that the theory seriously omits other important causal factors driving growth. As can be expected, this omission results subsequently in a series of patchwork repairing. Some of such repair work resorts to a "reverse engineering" approach (witness the many guessworks offered to explain the source of the Solow residual[2]). Needless to say, piecemeal engineering and reverse engineering are not good enough tools to save a theory or carry it very far.

Methodological difficulties apart, the neo-classical growth theory also makes an embarrassing metaphysical assumption. Since Euler's theorem tells us that it will take all of the output of an economy to pay capital and labour their marginal products in producing final output, nothing is left over to pay for the resources used in improving technology. Subscribing to the law of diminishing marginal productivity, the theory tacitly commits itself to the equilibrium paradigm. In so doing, it is compelled to treat technology as an exogenous factor. Alternatively put, a theory of endogenous technology cannot be comfortably based on the usual theory of competitive equilibrium. This puts the neo-classical theorist in a theoretical dilemma.

Even if we discount the technology factor, history tells us that the growth paths of many nations are beset with unpredictable outcomes brought about by contingent factors or events. There must exist certain pre-conditions that facilitate the kicking off of an economy onto a particular growth trajectory and making it "growable", as well as other contingent factors that alter its course of development. While we can concede that there are universal driving forces, which of necessity include factors such as technology (which is characterised by increasing returns), growth often remains a path-dependent and contingent phenomenon. Even if we succeed technically in incorporating technology into a broader equilibrium framework, growth as a complex phenomenon still requires more explanatory variables over and above technological progress. The diversity of growth experiences of different nations suggests that multiple factors are at work, some of which stretch beyond the economic domain, shaping a developmental pathway in a manner sometimes not easily repeatable. This is not to say that there are no universal laws that govern growth, but it is obvious that capital accumulation and technological progress are just among some of them.

1.2 Growth Driver I: Institution

Back to Growth Fundamentals

In spite of the numerous efforts to throw light on the phenomenon of growth, most of the findings are of limited scope or narrow interests. Some of them deal with issues of an empirical nature and are inescapably of local or piecemeal interests. Others theorise chiefly on the interactions among secondary level variables without challenging the fundamental inadequacies of the neo-classical core variables. As has already been pointed out, a lot of subsequent theorising revolves around the theme of "endogenisation" aiming to make up for the deficiency of the neo-classical model. Predictably, there is a limit to the usefulness of these efforts, for as long as these theories spring from or still stick to the original and narrowly based neo-classical arch-framework as a reference standard, major breakthroughs are not easy to come about.

Diametrically opposed to the orthodox theory is the heterodox institutional school. Institutional economics, instead of assuming stable preferences, rationality and equilibrium, challenges these concepts and replaces them by new assumptions of learning, bounded rationality, disequilibrium and evolution. The traditional institutional school emphasises the legal foundations of an economy (e.g. Commons, 1934) or the evolutionary, habituated and volitional processes by which institutions are erected and changed (e.g. Veblen, 1898). In spite of their valuable insights, they emphasise often on socio-economic rather than purely economic variables. Furthermore, they do not offer a systematic theory of growth, although one may cite examples, such as Marx, seen from the light of the institutionalist tradition, describing capitalism as an evolving and historically bounded social system, or Galbraith who examines the impacts of an evolving affluent society and big business (1958, 1963). Similar to the standard growth theories, this batch of "institutionalists" do not address directly the fundamental issue of the "grow ability" of nations.

Clearly, if we were to meaningfully connect the fragmented or local insights developed by the numerous researches in growth and development economics, or to provide more comprehensive or universal yardsticks by which future studies of these kinds are to be appraised, it would perhaps be more fruitful to re-start from a zero-base to build a new, general and unifying framework. The first step to take is to go back to the fundamental facts about growth.

Growth Fundamentals and their Operating Derivatives

As a point of departure I outline three fundamental statements about the conditions of sustainable growth.

Proposition One: Growth is a mass phenomenon characterised by mass participation at all levels of society.

Proposition Two: Growth is an inter-temporal phenomenon. Economic actors of different descriptions are supposed to possess the capability and the will to abstain from present consumption to invest for a return in the future.

Proposition Three: The future is and seen to be "investable" by economic actors. The operating environment must, to different extents, seen to be and turn out to be investment-friendly. Only when an economy whose future is seen to be "investable" is it in a position to become "growable".

From these three propositions, we can identify three operative concepts governing growth. From Proposition One, we have the concept of scale. From Proposition Two and Proposition Three, we can derive the concept of institution. From Proposition Two, we can derive the concept of productivity. Together, I will show that the joint effects of these three growth drivers go a long way to explaining many growth phenomena (which also cover development phenomena) and predicting the growth pathways of nations.[3]

Institution: An Introduction

The importance of the institutional architecture of an economy to its growth is widely studied and generally accepted, although the orthodox growth economist still prefers to treat it, similar to technology, as an exogenous variable. As a matter of fact, one fatal flaw of the neo-classical theory and its competing descendants is that they are deliberately ignoring the role that institutions play in fostering growth. One consequence of this approach is that growth and development are taken as quite independent areas of study, with development largely confined to the emerging nations.

Institutions, according to Douglass North, are the "rules of the game" consisting of both formal legal rules and the informal social norms that govern individual behaviours and structure social interactions (North, 1990). This is clear enough. But in the context of economic growth, I would suggest taking a step back and offer a more functional elaboration. As a point of departure, I would first relate the notion of institution to the growth fundamentals mentioned earlier. In this connection, I attempt to outline several important propositions.

Proposition One: The institutional architecture of an economy can promote but can also obstruct growth.

Proposition Two: The influence of institution on human behaviour in general and economic behaviour in particular, is highly pervasive, infiltrating and dominating. Conversely put, much of human and economic behaviour is governed by the characteristics of an institutional regime and is sensitive to any institutional change.

Proposition Three: The reason why the influence of institution on human behaviour is so pervasive is that the institutional architecture of a society or economy is not only hierarchically but also seamlessly organised at different levels of social and economic operations. This ranges from rules (constitutional, legal, regulatory) to organisations (the state, the government, the firm, industry and trade associations, unions), to other operating mechanisms (for example, the market, the franchise system) as well as to tacit factors (conventions, norms, codes of conducts, mutual trust).

Proposition Four: The reason why economic actors are sensitive to institutional arrangements and changes is that they are value seeking and property rights seeking individuals. They respond to the environment by formulating detailed and specific means-end plans to capture gains for the investments or efforts they put in. Any change in the institutional regime may therefore affect how they perceive the future of the operating environment and whether they need to revise or fine-tune their means-end plans accordingly.

New Institutional Economics

All the above are, of course, not new ideas. They have been widely studied and researched. New Institutional Economics and Behavioural Economics, in particular, have made a lot of advances both at the theoretical and the empirical level. Some scholars in these camps have also employed ample historical data to show how social and legal rules and norms shape economic reality.

There are, broadly speaking, two lines of enquiry. The first line of enquiry, which I would call the "generalising approach", attempts to relate economic behaviours and outcomes to different regimes, forms and levels of institution. It attempts to explain how different institutional arrangements impact economic co-ordination and economic incentives, for example, their aptitude for supplying collective goods and incorporating externalities, their efficiency in resources allocation, and their possible contribution to development (Hollingsworth and Boyer, 1997). However, similar to the earlier institutional economics, this new generation of scholars tends to blend their explanatory variables with other socio-political variables (for example, social contract, political choice, social justice and obligation) and call for more multidisciplinary types of research, so much so that the resulting frameworks often turn out to be broad-brushed and more taxonomical in nature. As a result of such sweeping and high-sounding discourse, these researchers tend to over-generalise the role of institution and its contribution to the determination of economic behaviour. In some cases, these researches lapse into mere language games.

The second line of enquiry I would call the "inductionist approach". It distils and singles out some solid and outstanding features of different institutional arrangements and studies how they impact behaviour. Paradigmatic examples include property right assignment and transaction cost (how delineation of private property rights affects transaction costs and market efficiency), asymmetric information (how asymmetric information embodied in an institutional mechanism affects economic incentive), principal–agent relation (how agents within some types of institutions hijack or abuse the trust given them by their principals) and moral hazard (how certain types of institutional arrangements encourage economic agents to take excessive risks) and so on. All these represent important insights and help throw light on how incentives and disincentives are formed and work. Indeed, as a result of these discoveries, the debate between the respective merits and drawbacks of the government and the market, including their complementary relationship, takes a new turn and becomes more sensible in recommending public policy.

In spite of these achievements and advances, New Institutional Economics has not come near to providing a fully fledged and unifying framework for explaining economic growth. It is true that since the late 1990s, development theories converge towards a systematic and institutionalist conception diametrically opposed to a "purely economic approach" which focuses on technologies, demography and markets. It is true that many of these insights have to do with economic incentives and disincentives, and have important ramifications on growth. Studies of economic disincentives also open up a deeper understanding of why nations fail to grow, or why the growth of some nations comes to a halt after an initial spurt. But a more comprehensive growth theory based on the institutionalist paradigm is not yet in sight.

A more mature theory of how institution impacts growth must therefore single out the most fundamental or "anchor" variables. These variables are then knit into a simple, yet comprehensive framework, whereby different institutional arrangements can be meaningfully analysed as to their roles in promoting or inhibiting growth. These anchor variables should also match the three growth fundamentals mentioned in the above, namely growth as a mass phenomenon, the investability of the future as well as the willingness and capability of economic actors to invest for a better future.

Risk-incentive Analytics and the Risk-incentive Matrix

The two anchor variables I choose for building an institutional theory of growth are risk and incentive respectively. It is not that these two familiar factors have not been extensively examined before, but they have not been specifically singled out among the rest to be erected to the status as the building blocks of an arch framework. By combining these two variables into a two-dimensional matrix, I believe we can more fruitfully explore their internal and intricate relationships. The insights so generated would enable many aspects of the growth phenomenon to be put in a new perspective. Taking these two notions as basic premises, I venture first to formulate the following propositions.

Proposition One: Economic actors are innately and naturally motivated to improve their lot by actively acquiring material gains and property rights, as long as the risk facing them can be reasonably gauged and ascertained. I call this the "theory of natural or endogenous incentive". The degree of "risk ascertainability" of an operating environment is, in my scheme of things, a prime factor governing the intensity of natural incentive.

Proposition Two: An institution that provides positive incentive for its economic actors and a high degree of risk visibility of the operating environment is congenial to higher rate of growth. Capitalism is a case in point.

Proposition Three: While in general some minimal level of risk ascertainability is sufficient to generate natural incentives, it is also the case that under an institutional regime of extremely impoverished incentive, such as communism, even a high level of risk ascertainability does not help.

Proposition Four: The level of risk ascertainability is determined importantly by the stability, transparency and enforceability of the rules that pervade all levels of economic activities. This explains why the rule of law, embodying all these three traits, becomes a bedrock institution behind economic growth. Factors that engender the rule of law and other institutional arrangements with similar institutional traits take time to evolve, for example, different mechanisms of checks and balances in society that constrain arbitrary power. Interestingly, technological changes, in particular modern information and communication technology, which unwittingly nurture more aggressive public media and a better informed public, exercise additional constraint on arbitrary power and reduce the impact of discretionary decisions on the part of the governing body. We can also expect that under a relatively stable risk-ascertainable regime, incentive schemes can be further refined and fine-tuned, thus enabling economic actors to achieve more specific ends.

Proposition Five: Thus the central issue about how institution drives growth goes beyond the incentive schemes provided for by a particular institutional regime. More importantly, we need to address the combined effects of incentive and risk ascertainability interacting under that regime. By the same token, any particular institutional design to be introduced can be similarly assessed.

Proposition Six: Since risk visibility and ascertainability by itself is so pivotal to economic growth, a fruitful realm of research would be to identity the various factors that affect this very factor. From a historical point of view, risk ascertainability is closely related to the stability of a political regime. For example, the extractive behaviours of the government on their subjects, notably codes of tax, are more predictable in periods of political stability. Conversely, the more arbitrary these extractive behaviours are, the lower the level of risk ascertainability becomes and the more dampening these behaviours will have on economic growth.

By the same logic, threats to risk non-ascertainability include the opaqueness and complexity of rules as well as the accumulation of semi-obsolete rules, which can be expediently evoked and interpreted by the entrenched interest groups of society to serve their own ends. The existence of multiple types of interest groups with diverse interests and strategies can also affect the degree of transparency of rules and renders risk less readily ascertainable. The greatest fear of economic actors across ages is, of course, the possibility that their possessions and property rights be wiped out totally and in a one-off manner during turbulent political changes or be confiscated under the whims of an extractive authority. No growth is possible under such a regime. Given that politics shapes what institutions a nation may have and institutional changes are affected by the political process, the right kind of political regime that can deliver stability is of paramount importance to the emergence of development-friendly institutions (Acemoglu and Robinson, 2012).[4]

Risk Ascertainability and Mechanism Design

If risk ascertainability or the lack of it is liable to unleash or smother the innate incentives of economic actors and is therefore central to economic growth, operating mechanisms which straddle different levels of an institutional regime and which enhance the degree of risk ascertainability can, by corollary, be expected to perform important roles in driving growth. Provided that the overall operating environment is stable and predictable, the prevalence of the right kinds of mechanism design can make a huge difference to the economic and business development of an economy. A paradigmatic example is the insurance system, without which modern economic development and modern business would have been very much retarded. Economic actors, being assured that the risks they are going to take are precisely calculable and can be conveniently covered at a known cost, become much more at ease in committing investment into a future that previously would have been considered highly vulnerable. This is particularly so when the possibility of a one-off wiping out of their assets or investments materially exists, for example, natural disasters.

Under the broad conception of insurance, a number of operating mechanisms emerge with vast ramifications for business practice and international trade, for example, a letter of credit that bridges the buyer and the seller at a distance with payment guaranteed respectively by their intermediary banks. Deposit insurance, for example, induces more people to channel their savings into banks. Different types of government guarantees perform similar insurance functions.

Insurance schemes apart, there exist different operating mechanisms that demonstrably expand business and investment opportunities. The limited liability company which caps the level of loss by investors and the joint stock company which enables investors to buy divisible shares are two important operating mechanisms behind modern business that have huge ramifications for economic development.

A New Institutional Theory of Growth and Development

Institutions are important for growth in that they are compatible with the growth fundamentals outlined in Proposition One and Proposition Two in the earlier part of this chapter. The prevalence of the right kind of institution thus constitutes the necessary condition for both take-off and sustainability in the development and growth process. How an institutional regime is conducive to development can now be usefully appraised by the twin notions of risk ascertainability and value ascertainability. Together they form the backbone of my institutional theory of growth. Of the two notions, risk ascertainability is of special importance as the ascertainability of risk alone is able to unleash a positive and natural incentive in the pursuit of material gain and well-being by the mass of economic actors. The economic history of man has ample examples to show how the right kind of operating mechanism contributes to great leaps in development (for example, insurance schemes), albeit more of an evolutionary nature than by design. The important point to note is that these operating mechanisms, whether by way of rendering risk more transparent, or of fostering a tighter reward–effort link, or of creating a closer tie between return and investment, can actually be designed and put into effect in different realms and levels of economic regulation and business practice.

Institutionally, at the level of operating mechanism and rules (which I now call Institution II as distinguished from the broad socio-political framework that governs the overall level of societal risk, which I call Institutional I), two main mechanisms stand out conspicuously in driving growth, namely the firm and the market. The firm acts as the operating agent of resource creation and allocation, while the market provides the most powerful platform for exchange in a world where division of labour and specialisation is the primary condition of production. The important point to note is that the market is not a static unchangeable platform that exists merely for firms to conduct their affairs. In the long run, behaviours of firms can alter the very typology of the platform, i.e. the nature of the market. As a matter of fact, both the firm and the market work in an interlocking and dynamic manner, meaning that changes in the "institutional genes" of the firm can have vast ramifications on the shape of the market. More on this later.

It is perhaps useful to point out that the notions of risk ascertainability and incentive go beyond the formal sphere of economic analysis. Risk ascertainability is also related to the general social ethos of a society. Economic actors, in ascertaining risk, inescapably take into account the trust factor. An operating mechanism to enhance risk transparency may be well designed, but often it needs some level of mutual trust among economic actors to deliver smoothly the desired result. Without some basic mutual trust, risk may still remain elusive and even the best incentive scheme may fail to work.

It is interesting to note that some scholars believe that cultural factors play a big role in economic growth. The classic example is, of course, Max Weber who upholds the importance of the Protestant ethics in fostering economic development. One recent study is Edmund Phelps's "Mass Flourishing" where he argues that the modern economy that arose in the nineteenth century was chiefly the result of innovation. What sparked this dynamism was a new economic culture, including ingredients such as representative democracy and a cultural revolution originating in the Renaissance, Baroque vitality and Enlightenment modernism (2013). While there is no question that cultural factors of such kind do make a difference with respect to the rates of innovation, they are, however, not necessarily essential conditions for initial growth. Cultural factors that affect trust, for instance, are important, but their importance relative to that of the right kind of institutional arrangements is often overstated.

1.3 Growth-Driver II: Scale

Scale-enhancer I: Factors of Production

One growth fundamental posited in this book is mass participation. Mass participation is basically a concept of scale, but the concept needs further refinement.

One can say that the neo-classical growth model is a model of scale, because it emphasises almost exclusively the importance of capital accumulation and by corollary, savings. Since both capital accumulation and savings are matters of scale, the neo-classical model, which is concerned with the quantitative expansion of an economy, is inseparably bundled with the notion of scale.

But the fact is that the notion of scale as a growth driver can be far broader and more encompassing than the notion of scale as espoused by the neo-classical theory. While capital accumulation and the alleged underlying factor of savings definitely constitute an important driving force, it is obvious that there are equally important scale-related growth factors. As a point of departure, it would be useful to identify a list of factors that enhance the scale of economic operation, or in short, "scale-enhancers" that drive economic growth.

The first group of scale-enhancer is, of course, related to the factors of production, notably labour and capital. In this regard, one may criticise that the neo-classical growth theory puts lopsided emphasis on the latter, assuming that the former, i.e. the workforce in an economy, is largely inelastic. While it is true that the workforce of a nation is generally inelastic, the rate of labour participation that is governed by socio-economic or even technological and cultural factors is less so. For example, the invention of many household gadgets which speed up the discharging of household chores, the emergence of the nuclear family, the rise in status and educational attainment of women, all contribute importantly to female participation in the labour force, an important growth factor in many nations. On the other hand, legislations like minimum working hours or unionisation can have negative impact on the level of labour participation. In the same vein, urbanisation and infra-structural build-up which facilitate labour mobility and the search for jobs are also factors that make a significant difference to labour participation.

Even in the realm of capital formation, the neo-classical growth theory is too narrowly focused. In the present-day economy with a highly sophisticated financial sector, capital availability is no longer solely and importantly governed by savings.

Credit-creating banks, leverage-providing financial institutions, the central bank and global borrowing all render capital for investment no longer confined to the habit of thrift. In short, the scale of capital availability since the appearance of banking has become incredibly elastic.

Scale-enhancer II: Connectivity

One important determinant of scale grossly ignored by the neo-classical growth theory is connectivity, which contributes significantly to the intensity of interconnection among economic actors. The number of transactions and deals made in an economy is governed not only by the size of its population, but also by the degree of connectivity among its economic actors. Con-nectivity, in turn, is governed by a multiplicity of factors. Of the many factors that determine the turnover rate of transactions, urbanisation, globalisation and information technology are probably the most visible and dominant. Globalisation, as a matter of fact, is a scale phenomenon par excellence.

One peculiar feature of connectivity is its non-linearity, which means that the number of transactions can grow disproportionately with an increasing level of inter-connectivity among a fixed pool of economic actors. In this regard, modern information and communication technologies, which vastly increase inter-personal contact, play a pivotal role. Increased contact among economic actors encourages the sharing of information and produces demonstration effect especially in the realm of consumption. Besides, the search cost and correspondingly, the transaction cost of economic deals will be lowered. All together, these factors contribute to some kind of "nationwide economies of scale", analogous to the economies of scale witnessed in the production activity of a firm or within a particular industry.

Interestingly, connectivity and its non-linear nature benefit especially nations with a large population. They enjoy disproportionately more benefits than smaller nations do, although the latter can reap similar benefits through participating in the process of globalisation. In short, the more open an economy is and the more it is connected with the rest of the world, the more it enjoys the benefits of connectivity.

This being the case, instead of being a seemingly passive phenomenon, scale is something that can be actively engineered. An economy can therefore be scaled up with respect to its level of economic activities. The extent of scalability is often subject to the kind of policy measures adopted by government. Thus, while a government has limited power to increase the size of its population and workforce (except by way of modifying its birth policy and immigration policy), it does have considerable policy space to enhance the inter-connectivity among its economic actors, and by implication, to scale up the level of their economic activities.

One manifestation of the contribution of interconnectivity to growth is the development of the supply chain. Supply chains are networks that aim at organising the most cost-effective modes of cross-border production by exploiting the comparative advantages of different places. They were first invented by the Japanese when the latter adopted Henry Ford's assembly line, added just-in-time inventory management, expanded the supply chain to include clusters of suppliers. This mode of operation was subsequently adopted by the "Four Dragons" and the "Four Tigers" (Sheng, 2012).

Scale, Cost and Growth

Apart from raising the mere size of its production inputs, scale also affects growth by altering the structure of cost. First is the economies generated, which manifest not only at the level of the firm, but also at the level of the industry and for that matter, at the nationwide or even global level. Other things being equal, lowered unit cost of production would result in higher demand on the part of the buyer and growing competitive power on the part of the firm, creating favourable conditions for further growth.

A second route is the reduction of transaction cost via improved inter-connectivity among economic actors. Apart from the introduction of more business-friendly and deal-friendly rules and regulations, an effective way to reduce transaction cost is to enhance the volume of contacts among the mass actors. As has been mentioned, this is vastly facilitated by modern information and communication technology. Not only is the cost per contact among economic actors reduced to an almost trivial proportion, the frequency and density of contacts are also scaled up to an unprecedented level, opening up enormous opportunities for information exchange and deal-making, to a point entirely beyond imagination by previous generations.

Other Scale Enhancers: Exporting and Entrepreneurship

Two more factors that can significantly scale up economic activities are also worthy of mention. They are exporting and entrepreneurial activities. Recall the rise of the Four Little Asian Dragons in the 1970s. Other contributing factors apart, their "miraculous" performances can be attributed to the exploitation of the strategy of scale, that is, reaching out to the world's major markets via exports. In spite of their small sizes, they manage to overcome the problem of scale via global marketing and exporting of their output. This strategy enables them to reap not only the advantages of cost reduction generated by scale, but also to expand the market demand for their products. The moral for a developing nation, therefore, is that whatever its original size, it can always scale up by integrating itself with the world economy. Interestingly, the value of exporting goes beyond the earning of foreign exchange. It also enables these countries to acquire and establish long-term competitive advantage over other nations in the range of products they specialise in.

Another important factor that can make a difference to the scale of operation of an economy is entrepreneurship. This is because new deals and investment plans in the private sector of an economy are directly related to the business activities of both the managerial class of its firms as well as its entrepreneurs. The entrepreneurial propensity or "animal spirits" of this group together determines, to no small extent, the investment level of an economy. As can be expected, major business and entrepreneurial decisions will trickle down to the level of mundane transactions in the product and labour markets with huge multiplying effect. The prevalence of entrepreneurship in an economy is governed by many factors, among which the risk and incentive structures conferred by the institutional architecture of an economy, again, stand out most prominently.

1.4 Growth-driver III: Productivity

The Misplaced Emphasis of the Standard Growth Theory

In response to the quantitative bias of the neo-classical growth theory, subsequent theories which aim at making up for this deficiency adopt a more liberal and qualitative approach. On the part of capital, they emphasise technological progress instead of mere capital accumulation. On the part of labour, they introduce the concept of human capital as a counterpart to the concept of physical capital, which emphasises the quality of labour rather than the mere size of the labour force. Together, these two qualitative factors, namely technological progress and human capital formation, are seen to constitute a robust driving force behind productivity growth, which is in turn considered to be one important spearhead of economic growth.

All this looks good enough, but the spectre of quantitative pursuit in growth theorising remains. In spite of their new emphasis on factors chiefly of a qualitative nature, many growth theorists are still keen on quantifying their respective value and contribution. In fact, one of their favoured directions of enquiry is to determine the proportion of contributions to growth by the quantitative factors and their qualitative counterparts. While this mode of analysis is interesting and challenging, the approach, in spite of the sophisticated techniques being applied, does not bring about very fruitful or even meaningful insights. The reason is this. The relationships between capital accumulation, technological progress and human capital formation are seamlessly interlocked in a multiplicity of causal directions. Until these interlocking interactions and their causal chains are well articulated, attempts to measure their respective quantitative impacts cannot bring us very far.

That productivity growth boosts economic growth is self-explanatory, almost to the point of being tautological. The more fruitful direction of enquiry, instead, is that of identifying and analysing the factors that propel productivity growth, in particular, the intricate relationships that exist not merely among the set of three factors now considered equally essential (i.e., capital accumulation, human capital formation and technological progress), but also between this very set of factors and the institutional architecture as well as the scalability of an economy.

In this regard, I propose a new focal point of enquiry by way of identifying two productivity chains. The first one runs bottom-up from the level of the individual economic actor to the level of the state (government), while the second one flows top-down from the level of macro-governance to the level of individual incentive and capability. I will examine how productivity growth is generated via these two chains.

Productivity Chain I: Top-down Chain

Needless to say, a properly functioning government at the top of the chain is essential. Basically a government is in a position to provide three types of infrastructure that boost productivity growth, namely institutional infrastructure, physical infrastructure and knowledge infrastructure. First and foremost is a mature constitutional, legal and regulatory framework which serves to safeguard the investability of the future. This is of primary importance, without which lower level institutions such as the firm can hardly work effectively and make commitments for the future. Besides playing a relatively "passive" role by way of overseeing a sound legal and regulatory framework, the government can at times help create Institution II mechanisms such as new markets through fiscal and industrial policies. In the realm of knowledge infrastructure, the provision of formal education at all levels (including vocational training and retraining) as well as the undertaking of or subsidising research and development are important measures that boost productivity growth. Government provision of physical infrastructure, which enhances the level of inter-connectivity among its economic actors, can also have strong demonstration effect that encourages economy-wide transactions and deals.

Down to the level of the market, competition that prevails compels firms to enhance their core competence and strengthen their competitive power. In order to stay in the game, a firm invariably makes investments either by way of expanding its physical stock and scale of operation, or by fostering product development or process innovation. In addition, by training its workforce or by eliminating its less desirable elements, a firm upgrades the quality of human resources not only for itself but unwittingly also for the rest of the economy through spill-over effects. In all these activities, the firm constantly organises itself for effectiveness in a competitive market. Productivity growth is, therefore, not only the natural outcome but also the necessary condition for its survival. In this respect, the quality of organisation and management of a firm can make a huge difference.

Partly as a result of the skill-set acquired in the course of formal education, partly of the opportunities given for learning on the job, the individual through firm-specific experiences naturally upgrades his competence. In so doing, he has the opportunity to move up the organisational ladder or to acquire a new job demanding higher skills. In the course of these efforts, productivity growth is raised.

Productivity Chain II: Bottom-up Chain

The foregoing productivity chain runs from top to bottom, with the government nurturing and disciplining the market, and the market, through the force of competition, nurturing and disciplining the firm, which in turn nurtures and disciplines its workforce. The outcome is that, provided that each link is functioning properly, productivity growth will be boosted in due course.

But productivity growth in an expanding economy goes beyond the chain of "command" from the top. It also works the other way round, with the individuals acting spontaneously as they strive to improve their standard of living. According to my theory of natural incentive, provided that the future is perceived to be investable, individuals invariably make means-end plans for their future. They would take initiatives to improve their skills in order to attain the ends they set out for themselves. Through mass formal education and continuing education after schooling as well as the provision of professional training, specialisation of skills takes place at the mass level.

With highly skilled and highly motivated people entering the labour market, the firms that take in these skilled workers become more organised, better managed and probably more innovative and creative. Not only will the more successful firms grow bigger, some of the employees may offshoot to become entrepreneurs and set up new enterprises on their own. In other words, the typology of firms in an economy will change, partly as a result of the upward mobility in the quality and productivity of its workforce.

As firms staffed with higher quality manpower grow and become more innovative and with new entrants joining the game, markets expand not only in size, but also segment into more sophisticated niches capable of adding higher values. And with size expansion, growing profits as well as new opportunities offered by value-enhancing niches, more and more firms will engage in research and development in order to capture a larger share of the market or to carve out new niches with exceptionally promising profits. Competition thus intensifies and the chemistry of the market changes in response to changes in the ecology of firms and their growth strategies.

As markets grow both in size and in the diversity of niches, old rules and regulations may no longer be able to cope with new products and processes that emerge. New operating standards, which include safety standards, need to be set. These activities, in turn, impact existing regulations and the role of supervisory bodies, engendering demand for improving governance. As a result, not only does the private sector witness higher productivity growth, the public sector, in response to such changes, also has to boost its productivity to meet the rising need and expectation. Productivity growth thus works both ways, this case from bottom upwards.

Although it can be shown analytically that there are two distinct productivity chains at work, in practice all the factors concerned impact one another multi-dimensionally in a web-like manner. In other words, as an economy undergoes expansion, a tight and seamless causal "productivity web" works in a self-bootstrapping and self-sustaining manner. But the working of this causal web is not entirely spontaneous. It depends on an exterior institutional architecture for sustainability. However, once in full swing, the causal web stands a good chance of further improving the favourable institutional and governance framework it once so critically depended upon for its kicking off. That is, once the right kind of institutional architecture is in place, we can expect the productivity causal web to unleash its bootstrapping potential. And in the course of its working, expansion in size will generate further scale effects. With the scaling up of the economy, more opportunities are opened up for the individual and the firm. The gains and profits they make encourage them to make more investment into the future, which in turn acts to boost productivity growth.

In short, provided that the institutional architecture of an economy is initially friendly to investment into the future, the three drivers of growth (institution, scale and productivity) will not only set off an interactive process working hand in hand in a positive feedback loop, but also improve the very institutional architecture that it starts with.[5]

Since societal risk and incentive structures play a pivotal role in the embryonic stage of the economic development of a nation, the quality of institutions makes a huge difference. This helps explain why early growth inescapably takes on a qualitative character. This does not mean that quantitative expansion, or for that matter, quantitative measurement is not important, but it is clear we should first address the qualitative aspects of development, i.e. the mechanisms underlying the causal web of growth drivers, before making attempts to quantify their relationships or quantitatively test such relationships.

1.5 Explaining Growth Phenomena

I have, in the foregoing discussion, offered a "tripartite" framework of growth drivers and analysed how they work in boosting economic growth and development. I have also advanced the twin notions of risk ascertainability and value ascertainability, upon which the tripartite framework and the underlying growth fundamentals can be interwoven and made more theoretically robust. Mass participation, the investability of the future, as well as the willingness of economic actors to invest into the future, all these growth fundamentals are deeply and intricately related to the three growth drivers namely, institution, scale and productivity. In this section, I will apply this framework to examine its ramifications and to explain different growth phenomena.

Government as the Arch Growth Driver

One interesting implication is that although I start with a "tripartite" framework of growth drivers comprising institution, scale and productivity, I will end up by adding another growth driver, one that can tower above the rest, namely, the government. I want to add that if a government chooses, it can position itself as the arch growth driver, spurring the other three growth drivers, which in turn, drive the economy to ever higher levels of growth.

The government can become the arch driver because it can design and initiate institutional changes, actively expand the scale of operation of an economy and foster productivity growth. In terms of the growth fundamentals outlined earlier in this book, the government can spur the mass to action, make the future investment-friendly and create a favourable operating environment, whereby its economic actors are both willing and able to make investments into the future. Alternatively put, both the economic environment and its players are in principle malleable enough for the government to work upon. The remaining question is what features a government must possess or what it must do in order to deliver the promise of growth.

In order to play the role of the arch growth driver, the government is well advised to comply with the following conditions.

a   It needs to maintain political and social stability, without which risk ascertainability would be difficult. This has serious implications for the investability of the future and by corollary, for the conferring of incentive on the individual.
b   It needs to be development-conscious. That is, it must have the will to implement the necessary reforms towards building an investment-friendly environment, however big the obstacles may be.
c   It needs to address different kinds of government failure in order to provide reasonably good governance. Good governance goes a long way to enhancing risk ascertainability and correspondingly, the incentive of its economic players to upgrade their capability and to make investments.
d   It needs to adopt the right kind of growth strategies, including the building of institutions that promote risk ascertainability and investment incentive, the enhancement of the scale of operation of the economy as well as the fostering of productivity growth.

It should be quite clear from these criteria why some emerging nations succeed in achieving phenomenal growth in the post-World War II era. The motives for fostering development are, of course, manifold. Some nations seek to develop because they are compelled to respond to the democratic demand of their increasingly enlightened citizenry. Some, inspired by the success stories of the industrial nations, are driven by their nationalistic mandate to catch up with the latter. Others develop as a result of the initiatives taken by the more advanced nations out of the latter's own interests. Whatever the reason, virtually most governments of these nations undertake different development experiments. Expectedly, governments who pursue policy measures that match well with the above-mentioned criteria score greater success than the others. Few governments do all the right things, but as long as they are close enough to nurturing some of the conditions outlined, they are well set on the development pathway. Bluntly put, development and growth can ultimately be a matter of government choice, the more so if some of the necessary ingredients of growth are already in place in these economies.

The choices that are open to government as the arch growth driver consist in four dimensions, namely, the foundational institutional framework, its mechanism designs, its policy measures as well as the quality of governance. Of paramount importance is, of course, the choice of the basic institutional framework, in particular whether the government chooses a command system or the market system. With hindsight we now know that a purely command system can hardly deliver the results we want. On the other hand, the market system, left entirely on its own, is also fraught with failures of different descriptions. As a result, much room is left in the government at the level of mechanism designs, policy measures as well as governance quality. Quality of governance, being culture related, is not readily realisable and takes a long time to develop. Policy measures, while easier to design and introduce, are often identified with an existing government or the ruling political party. As a result, specific policy agendas are likely to be ideology-driven and cannot easily last. The most effective agents of change, which tend to be more innocuous, ideology-free, and which can cut across different political regimes are mechanism designs. More of this later.

Stages of Growth and Development

The "tripartite" framework of growth-drivers also throws light on the stages of growth and development experienced by both the emerging nations and the developed ones. Similar to Rostow's stages of growth or Galor's "unified growth theory",[6] it renders unnecessary the artificial demarcation between the notion of development and that of growth. The former theories subscribe to the view that in the pre-development "Malthusian" stage, the benefits of whatever technological progress that may emerge are offset by population growth, leaving the economy always in a state of stagnation.[7] Such stagnation is overcome only when technological progress becomes capable of spurring human capital accumulation to the point where it offsets the negative effects of population growth, thus erecting a virtuous circle between technological progress and human capital formation.

My "tripartite" theory, while in general agreement with this view, goes far back to the institutional root of stagnation, take-off and sustained growth. In my scheme of things, Institution I factors that determine the investability of the operating environment as well as the perception of risk and incentive of economic players rather than technological factors, are the necessary conditions for growth and development. Given political stability and an institutional architecture that positively links reward to effort, it is only a matter of time for technological breakthrough of some kind to be attained. The exact technological pathway that eventually emerges, being contingent on environment-specific factors, may not be predictable. But given the ingenuity of humankind and his natural propensity to improve his material well-being, there is a good chance that given time and after a sufficient number of attempts, he may end up hitting the right kind of technologies with increasing returns that overtake the negative impacts of population growth. It is also interesting to note that the huge demand for labour, which provides the impetus for population growth conducive to the Malthusian trap, is a feature peculiar to the agricultural society whose seasonal mode of production dictates wide fluctuations in demand for manual input. The said trap may look unbreakable but lasting favourable institutional conditions that reward human ingenuity should eventually find a way out.

Thus in my scheme of things, the initial and necessary condition for development is the emergence of a favourable institutional framework. Granted that this condition is in place, the next growth driving force comes from scale expansion. This is to be expected, as some potential for scale expansion always exists in any economy despite the limits imposed by its size and basic endowment. What matters is how incentives provided by a particular institutional regime can unleash such potential and open up new horizons for scale expansion. Given the general scalability of an economy with respect to both institutional design and government policy measures (especially at the earlier stage), quantitative expansion as posited by the neo-classical growth theory should be a matter of course.

Since the expansion of an economy (within the natural limits of its size and endowment) is relatively easy to attain at the early stage of development, we can expect a spurt of growth once the economy begins to take off, bringing about a conspicuous rise in the standard of living, until the latent potential of its factor inputs nears exhaustion. How long the growth spurt lasts depends therefore not only on how large the basic potential is, but also on what policy measures the government will implement to exploit and stretch its scalability. As previously pointed out, the outstanding performance of the Four Little Asian Dragons is paradigmatic in this regard. In contrast, government policies that unwittingly result in de-scaling by way of say, protectionism and isolationism, may push an economy towards decline in growth or even stagnation. Argentina over the past century is a case in point. Originally a country that rivalled Germany in both economic advancement and potential, Argentina kept falling behind, thanks to the long-standing "de-scaling" policies pursued by its successive governments.

Once the driving power of scale nears exhaustion, further growth has to rely increasingly on productivity growth, consisting chiefly of technological progress and human capital formation. A special feature of this stage is the gradual slowing down of the rate of growth. In some instances, growth may even come to a halt. This state of affairs is sometimes depicted as the "middle-income" trap, where emerging economies that are previously enjoying handsome gains in growth somehow come to hit a wall and the economy may remain stagnant for an indefinite period.

One bottleneck of productivity growth is caused by the decline in the rate of technological progress, which is by nature an uncertain factor. Interestingly, one can observe that technological breakthrough becomes increasingly difficult to attain as the level of technological sophistication of an economy goes up. As put by Cowen, early-stage technological breakthrough can be likened to some kind of "low-hanging fruit" that can easily be plucked even by amateurs. "Meaningful innovation has become harder and so we must spend more money to accomplish real innovations, which means a lower and declining rate of return on technology" (Cowen, 2011, p. 20). According to him many of our recent innovations are, worse still, "private good" rather than "public good", meaning only few people benefit and the mass effect is diminished. Moreover, a part of such productivity growth is attributable to the financial sector which does not have much spill-over effect on the real economy.

In summary, the broad picture of development in different groups of nations in the post-World War II era is as follows:

a   During the latter half of the last century, nations in the third world are awakened to the need for development. They start to borrow and implement the best technologies and institutional ideas of the West. Taking on the role as the arch growth driver by their governments, these nations reap the benefits of "development externalities" provided by the Western nations as well as the WTO and start catching up.[8]

b   At the same time, nations in the developed world begin to experience a slowdown in growth, with rates reaching a plateau as they are exhausting their institutional and scale potential. They have to rely more on pro-ductivity growth made possible by technological progress and human capital accumulation. But unfortunately, many nations in the West are experiencing degeneration in their institutions. This is partly the result of their failure to keep up with changing circumstances, or of their "innate" propensity to grow more complex, hence more costly to operate and prone to abuse, for example in the realm of law-making and regulation. Since outmoded institutions are not easy to renovate and interest groups are generally reluctant to make concessions, institutional reforms for effective development and growth are hard to come by. Such is the case even for liberal democracies, which supposedly espouse the ideal of the open society. Institutional decay or degeneration, needless to say, retards economic growth (Ferguson, 2012).

c   As previously mentioned, some of the emerging nations lose steam and begin to experience the so-called "middle-income trap" after a period of fast growth. This happens when their earlier institutional reforms have run their course and the potential for easy scale expansion is nearing an end. Although there is still room for borrowing technology from the developed world to drive growth, these nations may run into two sets of problems. First, while they may benefit from the institutional ideas of the West and institute the right kind of reforms in the first stage, the quality of the institutional architecture they build often leaves much to be desired. They may transplant to the full the formal structure of the relevant institutions, but it is likely that they lack the quality of manpower to implement in a proper manner. Alternatively put, "hardware" institutions are easy to copy, but the underlying "software" required is generally lacking in the process of execution. For effective implementation, they need the proper social and cultural ethos to complement the formal structure of these institutions. Similarly, the quality of manpower essential to the nurturing of innovation and creativity takes a long time to build up. Moreover, innovation tends to flourish generally in more open and freer societies but many of these emerging nations still lack the right kind of socio-political soil. They need to transform themselves more thoroughly before they can produce, in a sustainable manner, high quality manpower with productive and innovative talents.

d   For the emerging nation, one effective strategy to foster growth and to overcome the "middle-income trap" is the promotion of the export sector. Exports can perform two important functions to overcome the limits imposed by both the size and the inadequate productivity of the emerging nation. Exports can overcome the scale problem for a nation once it successfully captures the world market as its platform for expansion. An exporting nation has to compete fiercely with other suppliers for the global market and in the course of doing so, it is compelled to keep upgrading the value of its exports. At the same time, the stringent standards imposed by overseas buyers also compel suppliers to sharpen their competitive edge by way of raising the quality and employability of their workforce through learning by doing as well as by importing more up-to-date capital goods. Once an economy has developed a robust export sector, it becomes much easier to attract foreign direct investment. Indeed, economies that register relatively higher growth rates often belong to the export-oriented group.

Analysing China's Economic "Miracle"

The past three decades or so witness a total transformation of the Chinese economy, to the point that its spectacular performance is often dubbed as a "miracle". While such achievement looks stunning, it is readily explicable with hindsight and is indeed something to be expected under my "tripartite" framework. Since numerous insightful analyses have already been offered in relevant literature, I will confine myself to highlighting a few key points, with a view to analysing two questions. The first is in what way the said "miracle" is attributable to the three driving factors in my analytical framework; the second is whether or not China will soon fall into the so-called "middle income trap".

As in other emerging nations, institutional changes, especially the market mechanism instituted by Deng Xiaoping, play a pivotal and catalytic role rendering the Chinese economy gradually risk-ascertainable and incentive-driven. With a centralised government having an undisrupted period of political stability after Deng, which provides a relatively stable operating environment,[9] China possesses the fundamental and necessary political condition for other growth drivers to work.

A key issue is why the development of the Chinese economy, which is still fraught with corrupt government officials and greedy bureaucrats and whose rule of law is still in a relatively backward state, is seemingly not obstructed by these negative features. This state of affairs, sometimes known as the "Chinese puzzle", challenges the alleged role of the institutional factor, in particular the role of the rule of law in economic development. The answer to this challenge is that although in principle corruption and the relative lack of the rule of law do discourage investment, in practice the cost of corruption in China is capped by the intense competition among its many municipal governments in luring investment. While investors need to pay an extra cost as a result of corruption, they can always choose to move from one municipality to another with more favourable terms to offer. Hence the risks these investors face remain largely visible and in my scheme of explanation, as long as risk is ascertainable, investments keep flowing in.

In other words, neither corruption nor backwardness in the rule of law (especially in the realm of law enforcement) in China constitutes a fatal deterrent to growth. Their negative impact on the economy is more than offset by the benefits brought about by the intense intra-municipal competition vying for direct investment from outside sources.

In the same vein, while some markets in China may not be as open and competitive as those in the fully fledged market economies of the West (due to the existence of a relatively large state sector with either state-owned or state-operated enterprises wielding monopolistic power within the domestic markets), the intense competition that prevails among the three hundred or so cities in luring both domestic and foreign investors (many of whom are targeting their production for export markets) means that the global market is serving China's enterprises well, whether they be state enterprises, foreign interests or private firms. This also helps explain why the rate of capital accumulation in China continues to stay robust. These cities and municipalities are eager to lure investors and offer them the best concessionary terms within their power, partly because the promotion prospects of their officials are tied to economic performance, and partly because they are allowed to retain a substantial portion of the revenue they generate for local use (including, of course, the sale of land).

The biggest contribution to the phenomenal growth of China is, without doubt, scale expansion. There are altogether seven factors that work hand in hand. They are:

a   Urbanisation – Urbanisation greatly enhances connectivity. China has been experiencing a fast pace of urbanisation during the past several decades. By the end of 2012, China has a total urban population of 712 million or 52.6 percent of the total population, rising from 26 percent in 1990. Between now and 2030, the World Bank estimates that the average increase in the number of city-dwellers will be 13 million each year and by 2030, China will have an urban population of 1 billion people or about 70 percent of its total population.
b   Infrastructure building – The pace of infrastructure building in present-day China is record-breaking in human history, whether in the physical or the communication realm. This again vastly increases connectivity.
c   Inter-city link – As part of its infrastructural building programme, China has built a huge transportation network of links among its three hundred or so cities. China's bullet-train network is now longer than all of Europe's. By 2020, the high-speed rail network will expand by nearly two-thirds, with the addition of another 7,000km (4,300 miles). By then almost every city with a population of half a million or more will be connected to it. This again raises connectivity in a non-linear scale and thereby the scope for growth.
d   Information Technology – The maturing of information technology, in particular the Internet and its widespread applications, matches perfectly the development pathway of China. This technology, by virtue of its

all-pervasive application in the realms of accounting, finance, production and marketing etc., enables China's enterprises to manage more efficiently their nationwide and international business. China's internet giants and IT firms, such as WeChat, Didi, Alibaba, Baidu, etc., not only facilitate business and consumption nationwide but are also posing a formidable impact on the world's internet business (for example Facebook's efforts to incorporate payments and commerce into its Messenger app are inspired by WeChat). Moreover, since this technology can yield increasing returns to the scale of its operation, and since it also generates big economies of scale for business, the two advantages work together in a mutually reinforcing manner. Thus this very technology fits best a sizeable country like China. Indeed it is inconceivable that China would have achieved as much without the timely appearance of this technology.

e   WTO effect – China has joined this global trading network. Partly as a result, it rapidly escalated the scale of production to the status of being the "factory of the world" via international trade.

f   US consumption – During the decade or so before the 2007–8 financial crash, the US consumer market has ballooned, thanks largely to the monetary policy pursued by the Federal Reserve. This timely opportunity is again seized by Chinese exporters.

g   Demography – Last but not least, the size of China's population itself commands huge scale advantages. The size of its population provides at once a large pool of workforce (especially surplus labour from the countryside) and a consumption market with huge potential. These twin factors naturally pose a great attraction to foreign direct investors with an eye to taking advantage of either its cheap labour or its consumption market. In addition, its gigantic size also confers bargaining power to both its government and its enterprises in matters of trade and technology transfer. Its large number of cities and municipalities also strongly contribute to industry specialisation that enables it to reap not only economies of scale at the level of the firm, but also at the level of the industry and further still, at the level of the economy as a whole.

It needs to be pointed out that these scale factors all converge during a very brief period of three decades, with positive feedback loops operating in an almost "explosive" proportion, creating as a result the most spectacular development story in the history of mankind.

Institution and scale apart, productivity growth plays a no small though less spectacular role. By all accounts, China is essentially a literate society, thanks to both its compulsory education system (in theory up to the junior middle level) and to the long-standing tradition of emphasising the value of education by the Chinese family. Thus the productivity chains analysed earlier work reasonably well in China's context, in spite of the fact that independent thinking and by corollary, innovative thinking of the individual may not be as outstanding due to cultural factors.

As can be expected, the huge size of the export sector in China plays a pro-minent role in enhancing productivity growth. Since the export sector is hugely invested by foreign direct investments, technology transfers that subsequently ensue also give a big boost to productivity growth among China's workforce.

To top it all, credit must be given to the Chinese government playing the role of the arch growth driver. Its will to reform and to develop, regardless of the wrong direction it picks in the early stages, cannot be lightly dismissed. With the direction of development taking a new turn in the hands of Deng Xiaoping, who espouses the twin notions of "reform and opening up", subsequent Chinese leaders have been devoting their efforts whole-heartedly and ceaselessly towards this end. Government as an input to growth, whether in the form of direct investment, or as the spearhead of planning and policy formulation, is hugely conspicuous in the Chinese economy. There may be big vicissitudes in performances and outcomes, but the will and pragmatism of the Chinese government to develop remains unaltered. Specifically worthy of mention are the many innovative mechanisms that span over the different ruling regimes since the opening of China after 1978. These mechanisms enabled policy-makers to get around the basic institutional constraints that were still prevailing in the transition of the Chinese economy from a command system to a semi-market system. These included the household responsibility system (HRS), the township and village enterprises (TVE), special economic zones (SEZ) and land leasing system introduced under the governance of Deng Xiaoping as well as the split tax system between the central and municipal governments introduced by Zhu Rongji. In general, these ideology-free mechanisms have more effective and significant impacts on the behaviours of economic actors and tend to survive different government regimes.

The important and interesting question facing us is, of course, whether or not China will hit the "development wall" or alternatively put, fall into the "middle-income trap". What will happen as its scale effects (including an ageing population), many of which are one-off in nature, become gradually exhausted, or as its institutions undergo stagnation or even degeneration with its vested interests defending their earlier gains, or as its institutional changes fail to match the new economic reality it has created?

My answers are twofold. First, even if the middle-income trap will even-tually come about, it will take some considerable time to materialise. This is because as things presently stand, the scale potential remains to be exhausted. There is still, for example, ample room for urbanisation with vast implications for connectivity enhancement among its economic players. It is true that increasing investment in infrastructure building (for example, transportation facilities linking cities and municipalities) will yield diminishing return, but some room for expansion still exists as urbanisation proceeds. It is also true that overcapacities exist in many industries and expansion has overshot in some sectors, but these are more of a cyclical nature.

That said, there is still a natural limit to the scalability of any economy. Even if the Chinese economy manages to escape from the trap, it will eventually hit some kind of a natural "scale ceiling" more or less in line with the experiences of other developed nations. In the case of China which faces an ageing population and is being haunted by the shortage of water and other energy resources, the ceiling may come unexpectedly early should the government fail to tackle these fundamental problems in time.

Thus, whether or not China can escape from the trap depends critically on its productivity growth, in a way similar to the Western nations when their scale potential becomes exhausted. Since productivity growth is governed predominantly by the quality of its institutions, apart from the quality of its workforce, a prognosis of China's future growth is very much affected by how we assess these factors. Recall the two-way productivity growth chains in my analytical scheme, where China seems to fare reasonably well. Consider the gradual upgrading of the quality of China's workforce as a result of its increasing spending on education, the continued discipline imposed on the workers by the firm facing competition in markets, its extensive deployment of the Internet, as well as a robust export sector seemingly capable of sustaining growth. On these premises, we cannot see why the productivity chains of China will deteriorate, in spite of the fact that the creativity factor, which is the key to innovation and which thrives mostly in a traditionally open and free society, may still be missing.

There are two more positive factors to consider. One is the unbent attitude of the Chinese government, who takes on the role as the arch growth driver. It is only reasonable to expect that, in the event of a sustained stagnation, the Chinese government will adopt whatever policy measures that may be required to address the problem, although setbacks and unintended consequences of one form or another may prevail.

Secondly, we tend to assume that all countries are alike. This is clearly not so. The likelihood of a country falling into the said trap might be importantly affected by the scale and the diversity of its economic activities which vary among different countries. The larger the scale and the more diversified and segmented its structure, the less likely an entire economy will be simultaneously trapped, leaving no room whatsoever for some of its less afflicted sectors to lift the rest out of the predicament. There is no country in the history of man that rivals the scale potential of China, in particular the unprecedented level of connectivity that engenders among its economic actors. Given that scalability is engineerable to some extent, the immense interactions among its myriads of players and its many heterogeneous sectors within which the latter can move in and out, may generate an unexpected level of synergy which, together with a determined government, may hopefully arrest China from falling into a long-term stagnation trap.

Notes

1 It is also interpreted and defined as the growth rate of output not explained by the share-weighted growth rates of the inputs (factors of production).
2 See Jonathan Schlefer (2012).

3 Amartya Sen points out that economic growth is one aspect of the process of economic development, which covers both qualitative and quantitative changes in the economy.

4 "Political determinism" is valid only up to a point. After political stability lasts for a long-stretched period in a nation, and sufficiently long to engender favourable growth factors, the accompanying economic institutions and the new economic classes that rise as a result may eventually become empowered to act as checks and balances to large vicissitudes in politics and its arbitrary, extractive power. This would protect the fruits of economic growth of the mass and send the nation to a trajectory of relative political stability, particularly if "inclusive political institutions" can be simultaneously developed. Whether or not these growth-friendly institutions will at a later stage experience decay and spur new political conflicts as the economy matures is another issue.

5 Some scholars, e.g. Rajan (2010), are of the opinion that it is too easy to over-value the importance of institutions. They argue that institutions actually rise in response to growth rather than the other way round. This view is open to two criticisms. First an economy may not be "growable" without the right kind of institutional soil. Second, it does not differentiate the lasting power and contribution of different institutions. It is, of course, true that growth can gradually build up under long periods of stability and the fruits of growth would gradually lead to institutional improvement. But then, further growth could be impeded if the institutions so far developed are not strong enough to withstand the destructive power of big one-off political turmoil. In other words, growth and institutional changes are a two-way causal traffic.

6 Unified growth theory was developed by Oded Galor and his associates to address the inadequacies of endogenous growth theory and to explain key empirical regularities in the growth processes of individual economies and the world economy as a whole (2011).

7 Classical growth theory generally holds that technology is a constant and that economies of scale are either lacking or of little material significance.

8 This is sometimes known as the theory of convergence, i.e. countries' living standard could converge in the long term if they have similar sets of economic foundations. Countries that share similar foundations tend to fall into the same "convergence club".

9 With the exception of the year 1989.

2   Growth and Its Consequences

2.1 Price–Value Analytics

In spite of the fact that economists as a whole try to persuade us that we are rational beings capable of judging for ourselves our best interests under all circumstances, the irony is that in many arenas and at different levels, we come under economic illusions in different walks of life. Economic illusion, in short, is one arch fact of economic life.

The causes of economic illusions are manifold. There are both objective and subjective roots. On the subjective side, these illusions are caused by our cognitive failings in judging value in spite of our beliefs otherwise. On the objective side, our poor ability to appraise value is often caused by the nature of the situations, especially game-like or game-oriented situations we face. In many cases, they represent the results of both factors at work.

In this book, I will explore some of these aspects and their ramifications. I will show how economic growth under the modern capitalist regime produces many situations that give rise to such illusions. The overall result is that in spite of formidable advances in information technology and our command of information, we have made little progress in dispelling them.

As may be expected, situations leading to the appearance of economic illusions are mostly the results of manipulation by economic agents, in particular, the government and the firm, each with hidden agenda to pursue. Some interesting examples are:

- Governments employ "off-the-balance-sheet" strategies to hide the magnitude of public debt in order to maintain public popularity.
- Pension systems and the way governments manage them often seriously understate the level of the long-term liability and affect the inter-temporal perception of income among recipients.
- Financiers manufacture highly complex financial products, for example derivatives, that lie beyond the comprehensive power of the investors who tend to under-estimate their risks.
- Exorbitant asset price rises leading eventually to financial crashes rather than promising a brighter future as many investors normally expect.

- Banks employ "off-the-balance-sheet" accountings and vehicles to cover up their real financial situations to avoid regulation.

In the following analysis, I will skip familiar albeit important themes such as how growth leads to the deterioration of the environment, how growth adversely affects the climate, whether growth is sustainable on the apparently finite stock of resources that our earth possesses and so on. In other words, I will confine my study strictly to the "endogenous" aspects of economic growth.

Value

Before I address this issue, I propose to adopt an analytical framework which I call "price–value analytics". I first deal with the question of value.

The notion of value, although important and indispensable from our common-sense perspective, is not entirely welcome and respectable in the formal models of modern economics. This is because the term signifies and embodies a strong subjective component that is not easily amenable to measurement and thereby does not fall neatly into the sphere of "scientific research". For economists who aspire their discipline to be "scientific", it is only natural they want to abandon as far as possible what they consider to be pseudo-scientific or metaphysical concepts, among which the concept of value, being rather slippery, is notoriously paradigmatic. I will show, however, that in so doing these well-intentioned economists deprive themselves unwittingly of the most essential academic resources needed to study the complexity of economic behaviours, especially in the embryonic stage of economic theorising. More of this later.

So, how should we look at the notion of value and make it useful for economic analysis? In a world of voluntary exchange, where give-and-take is the normal business conduct, we can posit that economic actors or players are basically value-seekers (from the viewpoint of common sense), i.e., they seek to get more than they give, though they are not necessarily value-maximisers. In a sense, human beings as economic beings are meticulous calculating machines or good "value accountants". We conduct, as it were, balancing acts and weigh costs and benefits before we forgo our limited resources for something we expect to be more worthwhile.

The value we go after can be material and almost immediately realisable (such as going out for a dinner, purchasing a pair of shoes, or going on a pleasure trip) or of a medium-term nature but also readily testable (e.g. hiring a helper, attending a training session), or of a longer-term nature (e.g., a club membership, a property investment) or of material but intermediary nature to be stored for later consumption and utilisation (e.g. dividend from holding company shares, interest received from bank savings, capital gain from holding an asset), or even of a semi-intangible nature (e.g. goods that confer special social status or exclusive and positional advantage).

Given the diversity of the nature of value and the different time-frames for value realisation, it is not surprising that economists want to subsume it under a simple, material and measurable standard. The simplest way, it seems, is to reduce it to "exchange value", i.e., to equate it with price. By conflating value with price, economists can avoid not only the most daunting task of finding a single objective foundation for the value of myriads of goods and services, but can also simplify their discourse and start building quantitative models without being held back by intangible qualities or negatively put, by "metaphysical garbage". And this sounds reasonable enough. But the price to be paid for adopting this approach is that economic theorising is being reduced to a "one-dimensional" discourse. The economics thus emerged over-simplifies the complex and multi-faceted relationships between price and value in different realms and types of economic activities.

The notion of value can be broken down into two sub-concepts, namely, expected value and realised value. Expected value is that which is perceived or estimated to materialise upon actual or eventual consumption. It is what is to be expected at the time it is paid for in an economic transaction. Realised value or experienced value is either what one actually gets upon eventual consumption or alternatively, the proceeds one obtains from a deal or transaction, these being "stored value" capable of being exchanged for future goods and services. Given the time lag between an act of purchase or transaction and an act of consumption or utilisation, we can reasonably expect some kind of gap between these two sets of values. Generally speaking, the longer the time lag is, the larger the gap is likely to be. In a similar vein, the more experienced the economic actor is regarding his purchases, the more likely his expected value will match the eventually realised value and vice versa. In addition, the more complicated a transaction is, the more difficult it is for the economic actor to guess correctly the realised value upon eventual consumption. In a sense, the gap reflects partly the natural cognitive shortfall on the part of the economic actor. Only in rare cases do the two match perfectly.

The Triangular Relationship between Price, Expected Value and Realised Value

Values, apart from those of an intermediary nature (i.e. stored value), are intangibles. Projected and expected values (except stored values) that are yet to be realised, and eventually realised values which are of an experiential quality are both of a subjective character. But market prices are not. They are tangibles, either as offer prices before actual transaction or as materially transacted prices. Transacted prices reflect the outcomes of balancing acts between supply and demand.

For any deal to be cut or transacted, the expected value on the purchasing side must be higher than the price on offer. Without some kind of expected surplus (i.e., expected value less money outlay), no transaction would in theory be possible, as no buyer would be foolish enough to wrap up a deal and part with his money without feeling that he gets more than he gives away. The same holds on the side of the seller. Since the expected value almost invariably deviates from the finally realised value, a state of natural disparity prevails among these three variables. That is to say, expected value is different but should be higher than price, and expected value also differs from realised value.

Since eventually realised value generally differs from expected value, one of the two following scenarios will take place. Either the realised value is higher than the transacted price or vice versa. In the latter case, the buyer would experience what we call the "consumer remorse", feeling either short-changed or regretting having made a wrong decision or both.

A buyer who experiences such remorse may either stop purchasing from the seller or he may still give the latter a further try if no readily available option is around. But if the same kind of experiences repeat, the buyer may eventually cut back on the amount of purchase or stop purchasing from that supplier. Should a large number of buyers behave in the same manner resulting in a significant drop of sales for the supplier, the latter may have to cut his offer price or improve the quality of his product or service. Reduced price either puts the expected value in line with the new price level or narrows the gap with experienced value. Some kind of equilibrating process thus ensues, manifesting in changes of demand and supply in the market.

Prices on offer in a market may differ from actually transacted prices, but generally they do not deviate too much from the viewpoint of the consumer. This is because the consumer usually makes the assumption that for any price on offer that they encounter in the market, some prior transactions might have taken place. Even if this is not the case, he still believes that the supplier would not set his prices very much out of line with the operating environment, so that prices on offer will become transacted prices. On the part of the supplier, he would generally price his products or services realistically so that transactions can take place. This results again in a convergence between the two. Thus both in reality and for the purpose of theorising, we can consider prices on offer and prices transacted to be practically equivalent.

The Cognitive Dominance of Price over Value

The above analysis is, of course, not new. Neoclassical economic analysis arrives at the same conclusion, i.e., convergence towards equilibrium in a free market, albeit in a slightly different manner. The main difference, however, is that in my proposed framework, the process of equilibration represents just one of the possible scenarios. Certain inherent biases in our perception of price and value pose a serious obstruction in the attainment of convergence of expected value, realised value and price. These biases also fall prey into the hands of those who find it profitable to exploit them.

While we as consumers would not part with our money unless we are convinced that we will reap a value surplus (over price), we generally take for granted that prices, regardless of occasional failings, do possess on the whole an inherent objectivity in the sense that they are objective yardsticks by which values, both of the expected or eventually realised kinds, can be validly judged or represented. This means there exists univocally a cognitive asymmetry between price and value, with price being unwittingly perceived to be more objective, more stable, more authoritative and thereby "superior".

Factors that give prices such cognitive superiority and dominance are manifold.

a   Values are whimsical and subject to frequent changes. Even the realised values of an article of the same kind can differ a lot if the consumption takes place under different circumstances or mood (e.g. having a cup of coffee by oneself, or with intimate friends, or with business clients can yield very different realised values). On the other hand, prices are more stable and predictable.

b   Prices are more solidly embedded in our memory whereas values, which are more of a subjective nature, easily fade away except in highly unique or memorable occasions.

c   Prices are generally perceived to be objectively rooted. People often look at prices and infer from them the relevant costs of production and thereby their "intrinsic" values. This sometimes gives prices an even greater façade of objectivity than the values realised upon consumption. More of this later.

d   Since prices are publicly displayed and advertised, people readily acquire the impression that they are widely endorsed or at least have the back-up of some public consensus. This lends an aura of authority over privately experienced feelings.

e   Perhaps more importantly, we do need a system of prices to nurture our sense of value. In a broad sense, prices guide value formation. Imagine we wake up one day and find that all price tags are gone. Not surprisingly, we would have difficulty in orientating our sense of value and would need time to re-adapt ourselves to the making of a new regime of prices. It is not difficult to imagine that the eventual outcome of the new price–value regime may also differ from the original. This small mental experiment should help show how dependent we are on prices for acquiring our sense of value (Woo, 1992).

We live in a world with countless products and services on offer, each type of product having a variety of brands in the market. To meet such a challenge, we need simple cognitive strategies, for otherwise we would be drowned by too much information and would have to expend a huge effort in ascertaining the true value for each and every product we encounter.

There are two basic cognitive strategies we tacitly and intuitively adopt. They are:

a   The principle of representativeness – i.e. prices broadly represent value.
b   The principle of proportionality – i.e. price differentials reflect value differentials in more or less the same proportion. Simply put, the more expensive a product, the more value it is supposed to possess.

Adopting these two strategies does not mean that we subscribe unconditionally and entirely to them in all our purchases. On different occasions we do fine-tune the details and question their validity, but on the whole, we do follow these two fundamental principles which guide our general pattern of spending. In specific cases where there exist serious tensions between these principles and the actual transactions, we may even go to the extreme of doubting our sense of value and accepting the ruling of price–value proportionality. More of this later.

Thus generally speaking, the basic assumption of the standard price theory, namely, price alone adequately represents value, does not seem far off the mark. Value expected and value experienced are come-and-go intangibles. In contrast, prices are more stable and more objective. By this logic, doing away with the study of value is not such a bad idea after all. In the least, it renders the study of our discipline seemingly more "scientific".

2.2 Value Hijacked: Scarcity Engineering and Price Manipulation

Soft Rent Extraction (Rent I)

The Advent of Affluence

Economic growth over the past two centuries brings big changes to the world economy, most notably in the rise of material prosperity. Increasing affluence inculcates a new sense of value among economic actors. Beyond the subsistence level, people look for other forms of satisfaction (e.g. Maslow). As needs are transformed into wants, consumption becomes increasingly subjective and psychological and even takes on a social character. Competition emerges not only among suppliers, but also among buyers vying for higher social status through conspicuous consumption, acquisition of snob and positional goods as well as enjoyment of exclusive services. Such widespread changes impact price–value relationship in an ever-enlarging portion of the economy.

The biggest change is that realised value can no longer serve faithfully and exclusively as a reality check against price. This means the equilibrating, triangular relationship between expected value, price and realised value becomes weakened. The agents of change are the brand builders and suppliers of positional goods and services who exploit to the full the cognitive dominance of price over value.

The Business Strategy of Price Manipulators

Brand builders using instruments such as advertising and marketing are shrewd in exploiting the power of price over value. If the average consumer believes that the amount of value embedded in a product or service is basically in line with its price level, the obvious profitable strategy to maximise profit is to raise price. But simply raising price is not good enough. It must be professionally and meticulously packaged because a competitive market will soon eliminate both the less competitive supplier and the super profit. Hence the supplier must adopt some kind of "monopolistic" strategy and deploy a number of marketing tactics that emphasise not only the outstanding features of the products or services in question but also appeal to the wider, intangible ideas of higher social status, superior life-style, peer respectability, exclusiveness, etc. that may associate with them. The business idea is to engineer a perception of scarcity and uniqueness and to balloon the expected value of the products or services by employing subtle cognitive and psychological cues, even if the associations between the products or services and these intangible qualities are only very loose or superficial.

The fundamental tactic is, of course, based on the idea that price has dominance over value. If people believe that higher price represents higher value, so much the better. After all, the power of reality check through consumption experience is not entirely reliable, if sometimes even irrelevant. If people cannot feel the promised value through experience, it is perhaps because they are not accomplished enough to appreciate the hidden or "intrinsic" value behind the façade of high price, due probably to their lowly status or inexperience. Rather than questioning the authority of a well-known brand, they would instead preach to themselves that the value that should be commensurate with the price they pay must somehow or somewhere exist. This is an article of faith, neither to be disputed nor refutable by "facts".

Needless to say, a huge gap exists between the prices that the famous brands charge and their real costs of production. Even after better quality, high-flying advertising, pompous marketing etc. have been taken into account, the consumer is still paying an exorbitantly high margin to the supplier for the intangible and snob value that they perceive or they are supposed to perceive. Alternatively put, in spite of the fact that the exchange is entirely voluntary, the supplier can still be said to be extracting a rent, albeit a soft one, from the consumer.

Under the surface of voluntary exchange, the reality check that can be exercised by the willing consumer actually ceases to function properly. Realised value as a checking mechanism can be very much weakened as a result of his self-doubt on the one hand as well as his faith in the "all-powerful" brand on the other. Under this circumstance, price–value relationship may no longer operate in a self-equilibrating manner. Price once set by a well-known brand hardly goes down, for that would be suicidal on the part of the latter. Of course, the brand supplier can still cut price on newly introduced products, but then there is still a limit to the amount of the cut, for the reputation of a brand rests ultimately on the exorbitantly high prices it charges. Given that it takes considerable time and investment to build up corporate images, successful brands are generally able to enjoy a strong monopolistic position for a stretched period. By contrast, consumers have only limited cognitive and memory capacity to accommodate the huge amounts of information circulating in the market. Given this asymmetry, faith in brands is, after all, not that irrational in our age of "subjective" consumption.

As affluence grows, a "trickle-down" process also occurs in the realm of consumption, with the newly rich aping the behaviour of the super-rich. It does not matter if the imitation is only partially successful. The process of trickling down is not to be deterred, even if members of the ordinary lot can partake only a small fraction of the dearly guarded value enjoyed by the rich. Satisfaction derived from consumption has become increasingly a relative and inter-personal phenomenon, with a significant portion of the utility coming from our acquired sense of superiority over those we know or even those we do not. With the advent of this "relativity component", value ascertainability, too, becomes more volatile.

The result, therefore, is a gradual build-up of an economy-wide drive towards higher-class mass consumption, as the trickle-down effect surges ahead. Never mind the borrowing and the debt. They can be paid off tomorrow when the economy gets more prosperous and when household income rises accordingly. Moreover this process can be self-fulfilling, at least in the short run, as increased consumption provides new opportunities for entrepreneurship and investment. Such indeed is the promise and magic of the modern consumer society. It is seldom appreciated that exorbitant consumption supported by excessive borrowing may leave these households in a deplorable plight in the wake of financial crashes and debt deflation, which usually inflict more harm on debt-laden households and low income groups.

Hard Rent Extraction (Rent II)

Growth of Big Firms and Rent Extraction

In Chapter 1 I analysed both the indispensability and importance of institution to growth. Broadly speaking two levels of institutions can be identified. Macro constitutional institutions such as the rule of law that reduces arbitrary power and thereby provides political stability constitute the necessary conditions for growth. I call those belonging to this category Institution I. But there are also lower-level institutional arrangements or mechanisms that are directly involved in promoting growth, which I call Institution II.

Among the latter arrangements that drive growth, one crucial mechanism is the modern firm characterised by the "corporate form" of limited liability cum joint stock holding. As opposed to the "corporate form" of sole proprietorship company or simple partnership company, this corporate form is institutionally equipped to become the growth engine of modern capitalism, giving rise to corporations with gigantic scale and advantage (see Chapter 4 for more details).

a   One advantage of this corporate form is that new shares can be issued by the company to incentivise its employees, especially professional managers and CEOs with formidable track records. Key people being strongly motivated by share or bonus allocation or share option schemes tied to their performances stand a better chance of leading their corporations to more productive, sustained paths of growth.

b   The advent of the holding company adds a new dimension to the scalability of the corporation and its power. With a corporation being allowed to hold shares of other companies, both vertically and horizontally, mergers and acquisition become legitimate business behaviours. Such behaviours are further backed up by the fast expanding financial sector and the leverage-using banks and financial institutions. The sky becomes the limit with respect to the size of a corporation.

c   As a firm expands, it enjoys economies of scale in its operation thereby reducing unit cost of production. In so doing, it stimulates demand and improves its competitive edge, which in turn facilitates scale expansion. A positive feedback loop thus emerges.

d   As a firm grows, it is in a position to recycle more of its resources for investment in the next rounds. As more firms within an industry do so, they may unwittingly raise the threshold of entry into that particular industry, especially for those products that by nature require a high level of capital investment. Heightened entry threshold may confer monopolistic advantage on the already established firms and generate super-profit for them.

e   As a firm grows, it gains more creditworthiness through its track record and thus has access to more or cheaper credit. Production-wise, this lowers its unit cost of production and helps further expand its scale of operation. Finance-wise, this provides the "arsenal" to engage in merger and acquisition activities. These processes feed on one another in an interlocking and non-linear manner.

Maximisation of profit or maximisation of shareholders' interest, whatever the subtle distinction between the two notions, means that there is no limit to the ambition of a firm. Under the present-day regime of professional management, which is another arch characteristic of the modern "corporate form", the remuneration of the management is often designed in line with the performance of the firm. To build up his bargaining power, it would be wise for the professional manager to create for his firm a steady stream of profit as well as to outperform his competing firms. Towards this end, the most viable and feasible strategy to adopt is one of "monopolisation". This is usually done in the following manner:

a Raise the threshold of entry for potential entrants. This can be done by say, developing or adopting technologies that require an extensive scale of investment, especially for products and services that by nature are prone to yield "natural monopolies" or by maintaining excess capacity so that potential entrants are to be discouraged from entry.

b Capture as large a market share as possible, even if this means lower profit or even loss in the beginning. This can also be done quite easily through the route of merger or acquisition.

c For products or services the operation or production of which requires conforming to certain technical standards, a firm can strive to become a standard setter. This can ensure the reaping of long-term benefit. This strategy is especially applicable to the so-called "new growth" industries marked by network externalities.

d Acquire large, strategic or long-term contracts from the government or government-sanctioned monopolies to ensure a steady stream of income.

e More strategically, manipulate government regulations and rules through intense lobbying activities.

This general strategy of "monopolisation" promises not only higher and steadier return, but is relatively easy to implement. This is particularly so with respect to lobbying activities. One reason is that bureaucrats are generally gullible (perhaps far more so than the consumers at large). Especially in the less mature economies, large firms find it easier to work on the governing bureaucrats than on the myriads of consumers with varying tastes. Some bureaucrats even take the initiative of meeting these big firms halfway. They may have been shopping around for the right business "partners" to reap a handsome spoil within their relatively short term of office.

Behaviours of bureaucrats and their impact on public policy have been well researched by the public choice school and there is no need to elaborate further here. In addition, the more resourceful a firm is and the more resources it puts into lobbying, the more chance it stands in attaining the targeted result. This again generates a positive feedback loop.

Price–Value Relationship under the Regime of Hard Rent Extraction

The triangular relationship between price, expected value and realised value takes on a new character under the above regime of hard rent extraction. Under this regime, prices are determined or manipulated by big firms (some of which are monopolies) based on a multiplicity of factors, for example historical standards, the bearability of users, the amount of rent they intend to extract, among perhaps some other equity and political considerations. All in all, there is a significant degree of arbitrariness in such prices, even if markets still exist and appear to operate freely. If prices are arbitrary, inelastic and are practically "givens", users or buyers have little room but to attune their expectations to the prices charged. Since there are few market options to compare and contrast value against prices, users have to rely chiefly on their past experiences as a guide. When prices go up, users can compare the differentials between the past set of price-realised value with the new one, but there is nothing much they can do, even collectively, to change the price structure. All they can do is to cut back some consumption if prices become unreasonably high. In some cases, reduced demand may not help as the monopoly suppliers may raise prices in order to maintain their level of profit.

Similar to the case of soft rent extraction which I call Rent I, the equilibrating mechanism of the market fails to work effectively. The only difference is that in the former case the consumer is free to persuade himself to forgo his bargaining power, but in the case of hard rent extraction which I call Rent II, the consumer is brutally deprived of that power. Under the regime of soft rent extraction or Rent I, the consumer may doubt the accuracy of his own judgment when there are big discrepancies between expected and realised values, but except in rare cases, he would not abstain from spending. Under the hard rent extraction regime or Rent II, the consumer, apart from lodging complaints, can seldom do anything effective to improve the situation. Under this regime, it is inconceivable that the consumer reaps his "consumer surplus", nor can he do anything over his "consumer remorse". In either case, real value becomes difficult to ascertain.

In a normal market situation, scarcity drives up prices. Under Rent I, scarcity is engineered by brand building and that scarcity is of a "subjective" kind. Under Rent II, the same scarcity is engineered but is now of an "objective" kind.

Interestingly, while economists are in full agreement that Rent II reflects a state of market failure, it is not clear that they would also see Rent I as another kind of market failure. The reason is that while Rent II is easily explicable in terms of the distortive effects of imperfect and asymmetric information, Rent I is jointly caused by the subjective and cognitive perception of the consumer and the seductive behaviours of the firm.

Since a "continuum" exists between the aggressive actions of the firm (i.e. hard rent extraction) at one pole and its seductive behaviours (i.e. soft rent extraction) at the other, the question of where the line should be drawn in defining market failure is not going to be easy.

2.3 Value Subverted: Financial Capitalism

The Rise of Modern Financial Capitalism

One major consequence of economic growth under the present-day capitalist regime is the accumulation of wealth in private hands. With growing wealth, the protection of property rights, including the rights to acquire, possess, transfer, exchange and endow, becomes the institutional cornerstone of modern capitalism. Not only have such rights become unalienable, uncompromisable and indefinitely lasting (unless specified), the wealth thus accumulated is also legitimately permitted to be recycled and re-invested to make new wealth without end.[1]

Wealth build-up in itself is not a bad idea, for thrift has always been viewed as a virtue in traditional society, and saving for a rainy day is considered a sound strategy at the level of household management. At the societal level, capital accumulation through thrift and savings is generally taken to be the key source of growth, as the neo-classical growth theory rightly insists.

As savings and wealth build up along with the growth of an economy, and as business opportunities increase, the urge for such surplus capital to seek a return through a proper platform or investment vehicle gradually grows. Since not all surplus capital finds its way immediately or directly to investment projects or the productive capacity of the economy, a portion stays in the banking system or other financial institutions and seeks an intermediary return (in the sense of stored value) in the form of interest from bank deposits or yield from bonds. With more and more surplus capital looking for a return, the financial system, apart from say raising funds for the government in times of war in some countries, is gradually transformed from being a temporary and relatively liquid storehouse of wealth to become an independent, active wealth creating actor in its own right, bridging the needs of the real sector and the idle surplus capital in the hands of the public at large.

In itself, the bank is a special "corporate form" that complements effectively the modern firm and corporation in the real sector in driving growth. It is characterised by a business model that profits by making ample use of the mechanism of leverage (e.g. mortgage financing). Macroscopically, the banking system is also able to create economy-wide credit through the multiplier effect.

With the banking system as spearhead, the rise of the financial sector becomes an important driving force of growth. It helps expand the scale of operation of the economy by channelling idle capital in society to productive use by firms and entrepreneurs. It performs the hedging function by way of offering insurance against different types of risks and hazards, for example exchange rate risks, thus enhancing risk ascertainability not only for individual deals, but also for the economy as a whole. The emergence of the stock market, which makes possible public listing of companies, provides in a sense a platform for easier risk ascertainability, especially among professional financial experts. The subsequent establishment of the mutual fund performs somewhat a similar function. Being an investment vehicle that treats all participants equally and that is transparent about its investment methods, it provides additional option for investment by the public, thus rendering value and risk more transparent. During this stage of its evolution, the financial sector serves the real sector generally well. As put by Niall Ferguson,

> Banks and the bond market provided the material basis for the splendours of the Italian Renaissance. Corporate finance was the indispensable

foundation of both the Dutch and British empires, just as the triumph of the United States in the twentieth century was inseparable from advances in insurance, mortgage finance and consumer credit (2009, p. 4).

This does not mean that the history of finance is all smooth sailing. Financial crises come in different forms and shapes. Before the rise of capitalism, crises in the form of defaults were caused largely by over-indebted governments. In the early days of capitalism, successive crises induced by asset bubbles began to appear with notable examples like the "tulip bulbs mania" in the Netherlands and the South Sea Company in Britain. With corporations growing in size, speculative euphoria may also develop when corporate cash flows rise beyond what is needed to pay off debt. Excessive speculative lending or widespread frauds triggering bust and bank runs are not uncommon throughout the nineteenth and twentieth century.

The Financial Sector from the Price–Value Perspective

In some of its sub-sectors, a financial market does look like a commodity or goods market. Both expected values and realised values are denominated in measurable monetary terms. This is particularly so with regard to fixed income instruments (for example bank deposits, government bonds and corporate debentures). In these sub-sectors, risk ascertainability and value ascertainability are generally beyond question.[2]

However, in the realm of variable income instruments and their different hybrids, risk and value visibility are more obscure. Holders of company stocks normally receive dividends periodically from their investments, but may stand to gain or lose as share prices fluctuate. Real estate investments share the same characteristic. While they can earn a steady stream of rental income, there is no guarantee of a finally realised positive return because property prices are subject to cyclical fluctuation. Whichever the case, the higher the risk, the higher the return should be. Since the risk profile of the individual investor, i.e. his ability to bear risk and his willingness to take risk, varies widely, there exist huge variations in individual investment outcome. Despite and because of such variations, the capital market works normally in the mode of an equilibrating process, with higher expected value and realised value driving up asset prices and vice versa.

This does not mean, however, that the asset market works in the same way as the goods market. There are fundamental differences. First there is a lack of the kind of reality check on the valuation of asset such as acts of consumption in the goods market.

Second, investors may hold on to their assets during a period of rising prices in expectation of further gains, thus limiting the supply available even as prices rise.[3] Third, many investors do not invest directly. They depend on experts or expert vehicles to do the job, hence subject to the familiar principal-agent problem.

Leverage and the Financial Cycle

Leverage and Credit Creation

Part of the reason why the capital market is normally characterised by an equilibrating process is that, similar to the goods market, households generally face a hard budget constraint, i.e. there is a definitive limit as to how much they habitually spend or borrow, which governs in turn how much they can invest. This does not mean that they cannot afford more in exceptional cases, but the rigidity of the limit is generally taken as a rule of prudence in household financial management.

Enter the regime of leverage. The fractional reserve banking system allowing banks to lend to firms on a relatively small deposit base is transformed economy-wide into a credit creation mechanism through the multiplier effect. As can be expected, this credit-creating mechanism significantly scales up the operation of an economy and helps drive growth. Over time, leveraging becomes the order of the day and eventually the cornerstone of the financial sector. One common mechanism is collateralised lending. Banks lend to real estate owners a sizeable fraction of the transaction price of a property using the latter as a mortgage. This also extends to company stock. With the arrival of the futures market, the practice of leverage becomes even more firmly entrenched. One by one, leverages of a higher order appear and operate in magnified magnitudes, such as derivatives and options.[4] Investors can now join the game for a very small fraction of the transaction prices, although they are held fully responsible for the risk of the entire asset values concerned.

Co-evolution between Modern Corporate Form and Modern
Finance and Risk II

The prevalence of leverage mechanisms opens up a new set of game rules in the financial sector. Leverage is inseparable from borrowing and it raises borrowing to a different level. Under the "conservative" pre-leverage regime, investments are mostly fully paid up and return to such investments in the form of capital gain via asset appreciation represents usually only a fraction of the total investment made. The situation is turned upside down, with return possibly becoming multiples of actual invested capital under the leverage regime. Investors now have two diametrically opposing modes of deciding where to put their money. The conservative ones may still look for stable return in the form of interest, dividend or rental income or some mild form of capital gain using chiefly one's own money. I will call this mode Finance I. At the other end of the spectrum are those players, notably corporations versed in financial engineering techniques, who look for capital gain using mostly other people's money made possible by credit extension by banks or other financial institutions. In these cases, the expected values and realised values of their investments can vary tremendously. I will call this mode of operation

Finance II. The widely accepted "mark-to-market" practice among banks also means that some investors can be granted additional credit on the basis of rising asset prices.

Of special significance to the development of modern finance is, of course, the advent of the limited liability joint-stock company, a corporate form that provides, on the part of the investor, a less risky venue (as a result of mechanism designs such as limited liability, divisible investment, easy entry and exit) and on the part of the firm, an effective channel to raise funds from society at large for productive use. The erection of the stock exchange on the other hand provides not only a centralised platform for trading but its listing requirements render the value and value validation of the companies more transparent. All in all, the enhanced risk and value visibility brought about by this corporate form and its impact on the development of the financial sector is highly positive to the growth of the capitalist economy.

While the limited liability joint-stock company is conducive to the healthy growth of both the real sector and the financial sector in the first stage, subsequent developments, however, bring about less favourable outcomes, largely of an unintended kind. One important landmark is the emergence of the holding company, one of whose chief functions is to hold shares of other companies. Since a holding company is legitimately permitted to have multi-tiered holding and cross-holding of other companies, some kind of "real-sector leverage game" comes into existence, incubating both the mentality for "empire-building" and the drive to acquire the necessary resources to do so. This structure together with the mentality engendered fits perfectly the leverage-exploiting nature of banks and financial institutions, and provides the ideal paradise for financial engineering, especially with regard to mergers and acquisitions. A kind of "co-evolution" thus comes into play between the modern corporate forms and modern finance. However, with increasing complexity of these corporate forms and their modes of financing, value and risk visibility are being compromised.

Another point to note is that the leverage regime in Finance II has the propensity to generate a self-reinforcing dynamic which lies at the heart of every financial crisis. Expanding liquidity helps drive up asset prices and investors reap handsome gains. With the newly founded optimism and profit, they are lured to take on more borrowing and channel more of their investments into the leveraged sector and leveraged activities. With the stepping up of liquidity, rising asset prices and player optimism fuelled by a solid reality check (in the form of actually realisable or realised capital gains), the original self-equilibrating market (i.e. higher price dampens demand and vice versa) gradually switches to an upward spiral trajectory, with super-profit in the form of leveraged capital gain becoming the fundamental target of financial investment. Over time, the originally self-equilibrating process gives way to spiral dynamics of increasing liquidity and rising asset prices. While hard budget and regulatory constraint or a higher interest rate may still exert some degree of countervailing force leading to punctuated periods of stability, the market becomes less stable with each new round of liquidity expansion.

To re-iterate, Finance II works in the following circle. Rising liquidity weakens budget constraint, resulting in higher demand for and hence higher prices of financial products. Asset price inflation yields higher profit for the investor, encouraging demand for more borrowing and justifying more loans made by financial institutions, resulting in higher levels of liquidity and intensity of speculation in the market.

This process has serious spill-over effects. The exorbitant capital gain via the leverage mechanism soon dwarfs other kinds of return to investment in the real sector. A sucking effect starts to take place. Not only is the idle capital in the real sector being sucked into the financial sector, but the capital which would have been invested in the real sector is also being lured away. Thus what we commonly call a "bubble" is in the making, i.e. some kind of lasting deviation of asset market price from its "fundamental" value. One may, of course, argue that increasing demand for credit would drive up the interest rate, which may then act as a brake to the runaway situation, but the gap between capital gain and capital cost is often too huge to be of any significant dampening effect.

Ironically, all of the above developments are common knowledge except perhaps to the orthodox economist who may still deny the existence of a bubble, and who may still insist that financial intensity produces valuable allocative efficiency benefits. As a matter of fact, some theories suggest that financial intensity can be rent extracting rather than value creating, and that any beneficial effect of increasing financial intensity in terms of allocative efficiency must be subject to diminishing marginal returns (Turner, 2012) From my price–value analytical framework, a "regime shift" from Finance I to Finance II can be said to take place within the financial sector, if and when return to investment in the form of predominantly stable income gives way to chiefly capital gain via leverage and asset price appreciation. It is not that market players have suddenly become irrational gamblers. In this regard, the standard theory taking the form of the efficient market hypothesis (EMH) is partially correct.[5] The players in the capital gain game are still largely rational players and they are indeed making the best use of available market information. In making investment decisions, they are taking calculated risks. Asset prices do shoot up in a bull market and in the short term and many of them do make real profits. In this sense they are without doubt truly rational "economic beings" seeking maximisation of value and return.

But the standard theorists are, of course, only partially correct because financial collapses eventually prove them too complacent. However, it is all too easy to blame financial crashes on greed, fear or herd behaviour, as the behaviourists would have us believe. So the interesting question becomes whether or not we can explain such phenomena on essentially economic terms without resorting to psychological or socio-cultural factors. In the following I will try to do so using my price–value analytical framework.

Unlike in a goods market, expected value, asset price and realised value in the financial or asset markets are all denominated in monetary terms. In other words, there is nothing else to check or validate value other than the manifested prices themselves.

In normal cases, value measurement in terms of prices should be objective and acceptable. But when price movements become highly volatile, the lack of a second checking tool of value can be critical. When prices are driven chiefly by liquidity which in turn is spurred by rising asset prices, some kind of internal circularity is generated without regard necessarily to the actual value of these assets or the underlying economic or business fundamentals. Moving in this circle, the fleeting prices thus manifested, while still displaying an appearance of objectivity, are actually built on the shaky ground of an abundant supply of liquidity and of a very transitory nature, increasingly divorced from the "fundamental" values of the financial products they are supposed to reflect. In other words, true value ascertainability becomes increasingly difficult with the advent of Finance II.

Not only that. The investor who relies on market prices as judges of value, be he an individual investor or institutional investor, naturally tends to mis-judge the risk he faces. It is true that on-going tradings in the market speak of the fact that investors must have some faith in the risk ascertainability of the financial products traded in the market, for otherwise such trading would not materialise. Besides, it is not unreasonable to assume that the average investor who takes part in the trading is aware of the basic investment principle, namely return to investment is commensurate generally with risk. If he makes a correct bet and makes money, it goes without saying that his faith in risk ascertainability is again well confirmed. Even if he makes a loss, he still believes that the outcome lies within his guesswork and is merely a matter of reasoned probability. It is quite unlikely that it would occur to him that there lurks another kind of "illusive" risk that escapes his attention, a growing macro-risk generated with each new round of credit creation and liquidity expansion in the system. This kind of macro-risk easily goes unnoticed by the average investor, as his attention focuses chiefly on the risk-return pro-portionality of individual financial products or groups of products based on such metrics as historical returns, price earnings ratios, book values, income streams etc. While many investors do take into account factors and indicators at an economy-wide level in their assessment of risk, such macro considerations serve largely a supplementary function.

In other words, two different types of risks co-exist and co-evolve in a dynamic financial market. We can call the first type Risk I and the second type Risk II, which more or less coincide respectively with Finance I and Finance II. Risk I reflects and measures the perceived probability of return or loss to individual or groups of financial products (loss being a negative return) versus their level of risk. Though governed by an array of different factors, this type of risk is normally thought to be ascertainable. In this sense, the Efficient Market Hypothesis on the stock market at the level of individual stocks' prices can be said to be partially correct. This is what Paul Samuelson means by stock prices being "micro efficient" and "macro inefficient".

A research study conducted over a large sample of US stocks by Tuomo Vuolteenaho shows that about two-thirds of the variability of individual company stock prices stems from responses to genuine information about the expected future cash flows of the firms and only one-third from changes in investor attitudes towards risk and time (Shiller, 2012).

Risk II or systemic risk, as is also recently called, is on the other hand, less visible. It refers to the potential risk of the market as a whole in relation to different levels and rates of injection of liquidity. Risk II can thus be said to reflect the "momentum" of market liquidity, which may conveniently be taken to be its mass times velocity. By inference, other things being equal, the level and rates of increases of asset prices as a whole should broadly co-relate with such a momentum. And by corollary, the level of Risk II can also be reflected by the magnitude of the gap between asset market prices and their fundamental values (or in short, the magnitude of the "bubble"). Although Risk II is often intuitively or indirectly taken into account by an average investor, it is likely to be considered as just one among the many taxonomical factors that govern Risk I. That is, it is seldom taken as an independent or systemic factor to be separately reckoned with. Thus when we say that the financial market is risk-ascertainable, we are generally talking about the ascertainability of Risk I.

There is, interestingly, an inverse and paradoxical co-relative and even causal relationship between Risk I and Risk II. As liquidity expands and pushes up asset prices, investors would find it easier not only to ascertain risk but also easier to make a profit, because the chances of their making the right bet in the choice of financial products increase across the board. However, they are unaware that as Risk I is going down and becoming more ascertainable, more trading will take place and the overall level of liquidity will rise accordingly. This means the level of Risk II (i.e. systemic risk) may actually be going up and becomes less ascertainable. As a matter of fact, it is the liquidity momentum accompanying a rising level of Risk II that enables Risk I to become more ascertainable and more likely to dip to a lower level. Little do the investors realise that as they are reaping their profit from a more robust market with apparently lowering risk, their growing portfolios are simultaneously being exposed to a higher level of Risk II. Being unaware of the rising level of Risk II and the potential hazards, the temporary gain they make from the lowering of Risk I encourages and enables them to inject more money into the market, fuelling further the level and rate of liquidity expansion and subsequently a higher Risk II. With this mutually interlocking circle and inverse relationship between Risk I and Risk II at work, an economy-wide euphoria eventually ensues.

Less expected is the fact that a rising Risk II can come to distort indicators used to measure Risk I, for example balance sheet information which reflects, say, bubble prices of assets. Wealth effects generated under the regime of Risk II may also be translated into unsustainable corporate profits in the real sector. Companies can also improve their earnings per share by issuing shares at inflated prices, at least for a while. In short, mispricing of financial assets can affect the so-called fundamentals. Understandably, the gradual dominance of Risk II becomes an important cause of failure in conventional financial risk management.

As can be expected, there exists a cognitive asymmetry between Risk I and Risk II. The asymmetry arises because while the individual investor is shrewd enough to calculate Risk I, he is generally unaware of the level of Risk II and its dynamics, to the extent that as he is gathering his "spoil" from a bull market, he may not be aware of its existence, let alone taking it seriously and systematically in his investment decisions. The main reason for the asymmetry, of course, is that Risk II and its dynamics, being less tangible than Risk I, are difficult to appraise and pin down. As mentioned, at the later stage of a financial cycle when speculative frenzy begins to take over, he may feel uneasy about the situation but still believe he is not going to be the "bigger fool". He may even take credit on his "shrewd" decisions as he is still making easy money, until the moment of truth dawns.

There is a further point worthy of mention. Relative to value, risk seems to be more difficult to ascertain by economic actors. This is in part the result of some ingrained belief in the "natural health" of the financial system and its existing mechanism designs. Apart from the leverage mechanism, many financial activities are conducted in line with mechanism designs that presume neutrality between debt and equity. As mentioned, one of the main purposes of financial markets is to help people to share risk and the financial system does offer products that reduce risks, for example life insurance, put options on a major index. But as Mian and Sufi have taken pains to prove, a financial system that thrives on massive debt financing unwittingly concentrates risk on the debtor, in particular households that can least afford to bear it. Conversely, "investors look to the financial system to capture government subsidies to debt. Many are lulled into a fake sense of security that they are holding super-safe assets, thereby fuelling unsustainable bubbles" (2014, p. 186).

So, how much rationality or irrationality on the part of the investor and how much equilibrium or inherent instability on the part of the financial market? While I will give a further analysis to the first question in a later chapter, my short answer is that the normal investor can be said to be acting rationally but at times under a "veil of ignorance". He is subject to a cognitive bias arising from the structural difference between Risk I and Risk II, the former being far more transparent and easily calculable. That is, his seeming irrationality at a later stage of a financial cycle arises more from his cognitive failing under an inherently volatile leverage regime than being the result of emotional factors like fear or greed, although the latter do play an important part as the situation worsens and is nearing explosion or collapse.

The second part of the question, i.e. how much inherent instability there is on the part of the financial market, is more complicated.[6] As seen from the above, the instability is due largely to the build-up of Risk II which reflects the momentum of an expanding leverage system not transparent to the average investor. Whatever equilibrating force that may initially exist in the market becomes gradually eroded when the budget constraint imposed on the investor is gradually weakened and removed. As Finance I switches to Finance II, with more investors forgoing a stable return and turning full-heartedly to the speculative mode of capital gain, Risk II grows out of proportion and the instability of the system eventually heightens beyond repair. The outcome is, needless to say, financial collapse.

The Advent of Hi-Finance

Economies around the world experience from time to time financial upswing and collapse due largely to the dynamics analysed in the previous section. In spite of this, the financial sector has grown increasingly robust world-wide, especially in the post-World War II era, as information technology becomes phenomenally more sophisticated and real time processing becomes widespread and universal. Part of the impetus comes from the huge amount of wealth that accumulates over a long and uninterrupted period of growth in both the developed and the developing world seeking actively a decent return as never before. While modern finance shares broadly the fundamental characteristics of the financial system in the past, recent developments in the last two decades or so witness some new turns.[7] I will call this mode Finance III or Hi-Finance.

FINANCIAL LIBERALISATION AND LOW INTEREST REGIME

Despite fluctuations, the past two decades or so, before the 2007–8 crash, is characterised especially in the United States by the prevalence of a low interest rate regime with far-reaching ramifications. This is no co-incidence. The prolonged low interest rate regime reflects the convergence of different contributing factors at the macro policy-making level. The US Federal Reserve, for example, needs a low interest rate to prevent the economy lapsing into recession and to keep the unemployment rate in check. The US government which becomes gradually debt-ridden naturally wants to avert high interest cost in serving its debt. US politicians, worried about rising income inequality, rush to please their electorate by pursing a homeownership scheme which requires the collaboration of low interest payments (Rajan, 2010).

Parallel with the low interest rate regime is the process of financial liberalisation, which has taken place in the US along with economic liberalisation since the days of Ronald Reagan. The financial sector has a strong urge to lobby for liberalisation and de-regulation partly because the huge amount of wealth that accumulates both at home and in emerging nations is seeking a higher return especially in a world of low interest rates. As a result of liberalisation beginning in the 1990s, big changes take place. Increasingly lax underwriting standards such as high-loan-to-value ratios and back-loaded repayment schemes appear in the mortgage sector. At the level of the household, mortgage credit apart, there is also an explosive expansion of consumer credit. At the level of the firm, corporate restructuring, mergers and acquisitions, leveraged buyouts and corporate stock buybacks – all debt-dependent activities, soar at an unprecedented rate. The Gramm-Leach-Bliley Financial Modernisation Act of 1999 which formally repeals the Glass-Steagall Act, allows commercial banks to take on investment banking activities and to affiliate with insurance companies as well as to re-allow mergers prohibited six decades earlier.[8] In other words within the banking system, the distinction between banking and trading almost disappears. As a result, the 1995–2000 period witnesses a dramatic concentration in banking through mergers and acquisitions.

With regulations suspended, competition to innovate intensifies among these new mega-firms, ushering in a new era of financial development. Alternative forms of banking by the name "shadow banking" not subject to the same regulatory oversight as that of the commercial banking subsequently flourish. Shadow banks do not accept deposits. They get the money lent out through other ways. Examples include investment banks, the structured investment vehicles (SIV), hedge funds and special purpose vehicles. The concern with shadow banking can be traced to the establishment of money market mutual funds in the 1970s (Admati and Hellwig, 2013).

OPERATING MODELS AND STRATEGIES OF HI-FINANCE

Apart from being spearheaded by big financial players, Finance III is also characterised by the advent of new operating strategies. One of these is the creation of synthetic financial products of different orders and types, most of which become increasingly divorced from the needs of the real sector. Certain financial instruments and vehicles such as interest-rate derivatives and credit default swap (CDS), as well as structured credit products such as collateralised debt obligations (CDO), structured investment vehicles (SIVs) and special purpose acquisition companies (SPACs) are structures of a higher order bearing increasingly distant relation to the needs of the real sector. Credit default swaps as unregulated insurance contracts, for example, are used to hedge against bond default. These financial products, especially the derivatives, go beyond the role of enabling financial institutions and other investors to hedge risks. They unwittingly provide vehicles for them to take on new, unrelated risks. With increasingly sophisticated information technology and mathematical techniques, the production of these products expands in an explosive manner.

Another distinguishing component of modern Hi-Finance has been the extensive and innovative use of securitisation in the US, taking advantage of financial liberalisation since the 1980s. Given that the traditional model of deposit banking has important weakness, for example disruption by runs, the difficulty or costliness of funding renewal or low return from investment, many tools have been developed to transfer risks from savings banks to other investors in the wake of the savings and loan crisis in the late 1980s, among which securitisation is the most outstanding. This approach was pioneered by

Fannie and Freddie. The idea is to group loans that are not directly tradable in a market together and turn them into securities that are tradable. A paradigmatic example is in the realm of sub-prime mortgage lending. These risky mortgages are pooled together by banks to back the issue of securities (CDOs) which are sliced into tranches by degrees of exposure to default, which are then given ratings by credit rating agencies. Investors are attracted to the "safer" tranches among these securitised products because they appear to be relatively safe from the angle of risk spreading and because they are endorsed by credit rating agencies. In addition, they offer higher returns in a world of low interest rate.

There is yet another change in financial corporate form, one that may well be counted as a defining characteristic of Hi Finance and that may have contributed importantly to the 2007–8 financial crisis. Traditionally investment banks take the form of partnership. Until 1970 the New York Stock Exchange required member firms to be partnerships in the belief that this mode of organisation is conducive to more ethical conduct, long-term reputation and trust. But since then scale expansion has taken priority and among major Wall Street firms, only Brown Brothers Harriman retains the original partnership structure with its partners bearing the risk of that structure (Schiller, 2012), the rest having gone public.

As may be expected, leveraging, both of debt and equity, in particular the former, receives big impetus under the regime of Hi-Finance. Since the margin of return to individual financial products is relatively limited, one logical way to magnify the total return on investment outlay is to increase access to credit so that the volume of transaction can be multiplied. This can be done by enhancing both the scale and level of leveraging, especially by piling leverage on top of leverage. The trading model of the hedge fund Long Term Capital Management that melted down in 1998–2000 is a typical example. Facilitated by the above-mentioned components, i.e. synthetic financial products and securitisation, multi-layered leverage grows with unprecedented momentum. Some institutions go as far as taking position with 30:1 leverage in the pre-2007–8 crash period. With the above-mentioned components working in almost perfect synergy, the financial system now becomes capable of limitless expansion without regard to or being constrained by the real sector. For instance, back in 1993, the notional or nominal value of US derivative instruments had been some $14 trillion. By 2008, it totals $600 trillion. No wonder the financial sector is, within a relatively short span of time, able to outpace by a stunning order the real sector in terms of growth and profit. It is estimated that over-the-counter sales of derivatives account for as much as 40 percent of the profits of firms like Goldman Sachs and Morgan Stanley. This results in fast growth of the relative size of the financial sector as a percentage of GDP in the industrial world in the pre-2007–8 crash period, with the US and the UK being paradigmatic examples. In 2006, global GDP is estimated to be $48.6 billion, but the notional value of all "over-the-counter" derivatives is $400 billion.

Each of these operating models and strategies of Finance III has significant ramifications. The adoption of the mass trading volume strategy via credit maximisation leads to a monumental build-up of debt for the sector as a whole. The mega-multi-level leverage strategy means that the basic prudence and accountability needed to protect the transparency and stability of the system becomes hugely compromised. The vast and almost instant production of synthetic financial products means that the financial sector gradually takes on the character of full-scale speculation among its players, bearing scant relation to real production and the needs of the real sector. Some of these products, for example the credit default swaps that are initially meant to manage risk, turn out to create additional complexity, fragility and ironically, risk invisibility. Similarly, derivatives result in magnifying risks, but these risks can hardly be seen by looking at the bank's balance sheet, and techniques to reduce risks from derivatives involve complex trading strategies which are often kept secret.

FROM THE PRICE–VALUE ANALYTIC POINT OF VIEW

One feature of Hi-Finance or Finance III that sets it apart from a financial system rooted in the real sector is its degree of risk invisibility. I have pointed out that an ordinary financial market rooted in the real sector is generally risk-visible and ascertainable, given a specific and relatively stable level of market-wide leverage and liquidity. The degree of ascertainability declines when the level of leverage quickly scales up and liquidity momentum gathers force. Under the Hi-Finance regime, the nature of risk takes on new dimensions. Securitisation facilitates not only the creation of multiple layers of intermediation, but also chains of inter-linkages within the market that render both value and risk highly opaque. Partly as a result, knowledge of counterparty exposures and uncertainty about whether those counterparties will be able to honour their contractual agreements when they are experiencing stress becomes hopelessly unclear. These features make the system more vulnerable to shocks. So there comes a point at which not even financial veterans can assess how much the products they synthesise really worth. Interestingly enough, one original purpose of securitisation is to facilitate the formation of diverse investment portfolios, hence for risk spreading. Now instead of mitigating risk through diversification, the exact opposite happens, i.e. risk becomes simply non-ascertainable.

The irony is that in the heyday of Hi-Finance or Finance III, mainstream thinking on finance, including that of the International Monetary Fund, is that financial liberalisation is beneficial to the economy a whole. It is generally considered, for example, that credit derivatives can enhance the transparency of the market's collective view of credit conditions and credit risks, serving both to determine the marginal price of credit as well as to discipline domestic policy. Such experts also note with approval that the dispersion of credit risk by banks to a broader and more diverse group of investors help make the banking and overall financial system more resilient. Also, since risk would be dispersed more efficiently into the balance sheets of those best placed to manage it, financial intensity would increase the stability of the financial system rather than destabilise it. They show great faith in the capacity of the risk management systems that are employed to cope with the increasing complexity of the financial market, which is considered at once rational and self-equilibrating.

Similar to Finance II, where speculation for capital gain using leverage and credit takes over as the prime investment objective, real value under the regime of Finance III also becomes increasingly less ascertainable. As asset price movements accelerate, Risk I calculations become dangerously irrelevant even as speculative trading still yields handsome return. In the circumstance, Risk I consideration pale into insignifance as Risk II begins to reign, regardless of the still solid appearance of asset prices and the apparent efficacy of risk management systems.

This is not to say that financiers and experts in the financial field are indifferent to the risk picture. Ironically, one of their chief tasks is to manage risk. Indeed, quantitative measurement of financial risk is all-pervasive in today's banking, asset management and regulatory systems. There are, however, four problems involved. First the "value at risk" methodologies generally employed, including those of major investment banks are based on the premise of market efficiency. They stem from the shaky foundation that the observed frequency distribution of market price movements in the recent past have strong inferences for the probability distribution of future movements and can thus be used to assess the maximum losses at any given level of confidence. This assumption, however, suffers from the serious flaw that the distributions are "normal", meaning the objective probability distribution of future outcomes from observations of past data can be derived. Alternatively put, it is commonly believed that reliable probability distributions for future asset price returns can be determined. Moreover, reliance on recent past data implies a systematic tendency to pro-cyclical assessments. But when the markets are caught in a self-reinforcing cycle, these distributions can fail entirely.

The second problem is that partly under pressure from shareholders, banks tend to operate with minimum equity in order to yield higher yields. From mid-1990s, they use, with approval from the regulators, their own "internal" models to assess the risks of their investments, meaning that they can set their own standards of capital requirement. As a result, their balance sheets balloon without a commensurate rise in capital. Regulators allow this in the belief that banks have more up-to-date information about these risks as well as better techniques for evaluating them, without considering the possibility that banks might manipulate risk measurement in their own interest. As a matter of fact, banks have developed various techniques for "risk-weight optimisation" that allow them to choose investments that are riskier than the supervisors would believe.

Third, the belief of bankers and financial experts that they have the ability to manage risk may make them excessively confident about their models and methods. The sense of control generated by the sophisticated quantitative risk management models they command may make even experts less cautious about limiting their exposure.

The fourth problem can be better understood by introducing the notion Risk III. In contrast to Risk I and Risk II, Risk III can be seen as some kind of global risk ceiling perceived by the financiers and governs how much risk they are to take. This perception is unwittingly inculcated over time and repeatedly by safety net measures adopted by the regulators in the name of investor protection, ranging from deposit insurance to implicit government guarantee to bail them out in the event of a crisis, for fear that the shocks that may erupt would be too much for the economy to bear. When the existence of "a rescuer of the last resort" becomes an entrenched belief (and also reality), the moral hazard of taking excessive risk becomes unavoidable. In the nineteenth century, when banks took the corporate form of partnerships whose owners were fully liable for their debts, equity level of the order of 40 or even 50 percent of their total assets were common. Banks today have equity level probably less than 5 percent of their total assets, possibly as low as 2 to 3 percent. Even Basel III introduced in 2015 sets the minimum leverage ratio, i.e. the relation between debt and equity, at just 3 percent (cf Admati and Hellwig, 2013). Needless to say, the lower Risk III is (i.e. the higher the possibility that they will be bailed out), the more the players are motivated to take leveraged risk. Alternatively put, the perceived Risk III renders the players less wary of the consequences of Risk II. Indirectly, it encourages more relentless leveraging and speculative activities which further drive up Risk II until the bust becomes a foregone conclusion.

The 2007–8 Financial Crash and the Aftermath

By now the story of the 2007–8 financial crash has been told and re-told many times in different manners and along different themes. Some of them are analytical narratives focusing on the cast of key players, exposing their folly, greed or conspiracies.[9] Some trace the developmental processes of the major financial products and the mechanisms of securitisation responsible for the collapse. Some deal with the macro-economic and global factors and events that converge to brew this "perfect storm". Some try to answer the intriguing question of whether this time is really different and how. With this rich literature, there is virtually little need for another conventional narrative or analysis and for me to repeat these familiar points so well articulated by so many others. I will briefly focus on a few controversial issues from the perspective developed in this book.

Briefly put, the 2007–8 financial crash is a full manifestation of the dynamics of Finance III as analysed in the preceding section. The most prominent feature is that while the 2007–8 crash shares all the characteristics typical of a financial crash, it is "perfect" in that all the conceivable essential components happen to be in place, although fundamentally, it is a massive institutional failure.

These include (a) a prolonged period of wealth accumulation coupled with a long-stretched regime of low interest rate fuelling a real-estate bubble and the need for high-yield financial products; (b) the build-up of a "debt culture" with encouragement from policymakers, creating both an insatiable demand for debt and the easy supply of debt under a leverage regime; (c) the "timely" maturation of sophisticated information and telecommunication technologies; (d) big gaps in the US regulatory structure with individual agencies looking at different parts of the system and none paying enough attention to the stability of the financial system as a whole; (e) pro-market regulators who blind their eyes to the explosive dynamics of Hi-Finance because of their strong belief in the efficacy of the Efficient Market Hypothesis (EMH), which is alleged to be one of the major catalysts of financial de-regulation; (f) the folly of financiers complacent with their way of managing risk and in their belief that they are successful in banishing it when actually they have lost track; (g) malpractices among banks, some of them even turning themselves in effect into hedge funds, making derivative bets against their own clients; (h) the inexperience of credit rating agencies in handling the assessments of structured credit products, particularly tranches of mortgaged-backed securities (MBS) and collateralised debt obligations (CDO) and the mistrust of investors in the formers' capability to make reliable valuations; (i) the American homeownership dream coinciding with its politicians trying to please an unhappy electorate who feel deprived due to rising income disparity, which results in extensive scandalous sub-prime loans; (j) the interconnectedness, high degree of indebtedness and the contagion mechanisms that spread losses, features that characterise a large number of financial institutions world-wide that hold huge amounts of subprime mortgage related securities; (k) the incredibly low equity level relative to debt, with some of the major financial institutions world-wide having equity as low as 2 or 3 percent of their total assets, bearing in mind that debt instruments introduce into the economy important potential rigidities, irreversibility and pro-cyclical tendencies; (l) the huge accumulation of foreign exchange reserves by the fast-growing emerging nations (the so-called "savings glut") all ready to feed both the debt-hungry industrial nations and their consumption-hungry people, and so forth.

The 2007–8 "storm" is also "perfect" from my analytical framework, in that the twin invisibilities of risk and value reach their heights before the collapse. With securitisation becoming the order of the day and as layers of leveraging are piling up, the system is building up a momentum and fast regressing from the state of risk calculability (i.e. Risk I) to the "deep waters" of uncertainty (i.e. Risk II at the apex). No one, including the credit rating agencies, who are supposed to know best, truly knows how much risk is out there. In short, "Knightian uncertainty" gradually reigns even as financiers think that their strategy of diversifying risk via securitisation is tantamount to reducing risk.

The situation is pretty much the same in so far as value ascertainability goes. As asset prices are supposed to be the most authoritative parameters to reflect and validate value, investors coming under the illusion of the solidness of market prices still believe or persuade themselves to believe that "real" values are ascertainable, even though they may be dimly aware that it is actually the rising and internally generated liquidity that pushes up prices. Unfortunately, the cognitive asymmetry between Risk I and Risk II effectively blocks them from seeing clearly that the prices manifested in the market at a later stage reflect merely the volatility of market liquidity rather than the "real" values of the assets in line with basic economic fundamentals and in a dangerously transitory manner. As a matter of fact, it is these twin invisibilities that explain why most of the financiers in the game are so deeply engrossed but remain so passive and helpless at the last hour when they know deep at heart that the storm is just round the corner. There is no easy exit because the momentum thus built up is not reversible. They can only carry on their game and play by the "music" of manifest market prices, taking comfort in their perception of Risk III, namely, the government will most likely come to rescue them in the event of a crash. The rest is history.

With the above analysis, I now attempt to give a brief answer to the question: "Will the next time be different?" The answer is both yes and no. Yes because it is very difficult to simulate all the almost perfect factors and conditions that contribute and lead to the 2007–8 collapse, especially as some of these are of a contingent nature. Yes also because the level of risk visibility of the system regressing towards almost complete uncertainty or metaphorically the "Stone Age" is probably unique and therefore partially avoidable in the future with a tighter regulatory framework. But then, this collapse shares broadly the salient features of a typical financial meltdown and is therefore fundamentally not much different in terms of leverage exploitation, liquidity generation, diminishing risk and value ascertainability. The 2007–8 collapse, albeit of a tall order, is therefore structurally pretty much the same.

A second similar question is "Will history repeat itself?" The answer is "it depends". It is true that since 2008, a mass of macro-prudential policies and rules have been instituted, including new tougher leverage ratios, thus boosting bank capital and equity. Should the tightened regulations gradually unwind with the fading of memory, the story of the financial cycle will likely repeat particularly as government support of the financial industry in the form of subsidies, guarantees or bail-outs remain unabated, encouraging unwittingly excessive risk-taking or in other words, as long as Risk III remains in place. But future ones will probably be of lesser magnitude, now that we have learned at least some of the lessons.[10] Just as we have managed to avoid in the aftermath of 2007–8 the intensity of impact similar to that of the "Great Depression", we should be able to avoid the extremes of the 2007–8 collapse in the future.

The most interesting and intriguing aspect about the 2007–8 collapse is not what causes it. By now, despite the diversity of perspectives, we have basically a good consensus of why and how it happens. What is more intriguing (and this time is really different), is the nature of the recovery. Why does recovery take so long to come about and why the recovery, many years on and after so much rescue effort being made, still looks quite pale and weak? Another disturbing question is whether or not the present recovery is costless or is it chiefly engineered by the huge government debt being incurred? If the latter is the case, is it a true recovery or merely a false dawn? To analyse this question, we need a broader analytical framework and need to introduce new parameters into our discussion. Again, this has to do with the long-term consequences of economic growth.

2.4 How Growth Subverts Equality

The Inequality Problem Dismissed

The democratisation of living standards has masked a dramatic concentration of incomes over the past 30 years. In spite of the continually narrowing gap between the GDP per capita of the industrial world and that of the emerging nations, more than two-thirds of the world's people live in countries where income disparities, contrary to the prediction of Simon Kuznets (1955), have risen since the 1980s. This also goes against the conventional wisdom that the shares of income flowing to labour and capital are relatively constant (e.g. Kaldor, 1957). There are two dimensions to this problem. First the "labour share" of national income has been falling across much of the world since the 1980s. The Organisation for Economic Co-operation and Development (OECD) reckons that labour in its member countries takes 62 percent of all income in the 2000s, down from over 66 percent in the early 1990s. Second, as the overall labour share is falling, the share of income earned by the top 1 percent group has, say in the United States, increased since the 1990s. Even more startling, the share of national income going to the top 0.01 percent (some 16,000 families) has risen from just over 1 percent in 1980 to almost 5 percent now. Even Norway and Sweden, presumably among the world's most equitable societies, are registering shrinking labour shares.

What is equally disturbing is that the gap widens not only between the super-rich and the rest across many nations, developed and developing alike, but that the gap between the income of the top 10 percent and that of the rest is also widening significantly, suggesting that a polarisation process is at work among the workforce of an economy, with the highly skilled elite group taking the lion's share of the fruits of economic growth. Little wonder Barack Obama proclaimed that inequality is the defining issue of our time.[11]

Parallel to the phenomenon of deteriorating income disparity is the question of increasing wealth inequality. Thomas Piketty shows that the rate of capital return in developed countries is persistently greater than the rate of economic growth over the past two hundred years and argues that this trend of concentration is not self-correcting (2014).

The ultra-conservative economist, as can be expected, shows little worry about such deteriorating trends. To him, economic inequality is neither something new nor has much impact on the material well-being of most people as long as the economy manages to grow. He might even argue that some degree of inequality might be useful in spurring the less resourceful to action, thereby maintaining the upward mobility of society. To him, income or wealth disparity is a pseudo-problem that does not have to be taken seriously. Conservatives in the nineteenth century even defended inequality and property rights as elements of a natural order.

There are, briefly put, several commonly used arguments to dismiss inequality as a pseudo-problem or to belittle its significance. The first one is the "trickle down" argument. The rich may be the first to benefit and perhaps take most from the gains of economic growth, but in the subsequent rounds such gains will filter to the lower classes through the "trickle-down" effect. This is because the rich, out of self-interest, will use their growing resources to make investments which lead to more employment, higher wages as well as technological innovation. The increased tax they pay will also help the destitute and the poor. Eventually everyone will stand to benefit.

The second argument, an extension of the first one, accepts the fact that the distributive gap between capital and labour may widen over time. But capital has an indispensable role to play in upgrading labour productivity. Since increased labour productivity helps drive innovation and make better use of capital, these two factor inputs operate in a mutually reinforcing manner in a free market, resulting in the bootstrapping of the economy. In other words, the collaboration between capital and labour represents a positive-sum game rather than a zero-sum one. While the present arrangement may not be the most desirable, any other distributive system, especially of a more arbitrary kind, would take away such natural synergy and do more harm than good.

The third argument is this. According to the marginal productivity theory, factor inputs are rewarded according to the value of their marginal products in a free market. Since everyone earns what he naturally deserves, this is by far the most equitable arrangement. Thus there is no reason to condemn the rich for getting a bigger slice of the economic pie.

The fourth argument accepts the fact that there may be repercussions generated by distributive disparity, that there are real losers and that the least privileged group in a society has little hope of surviving in the game. But looking after these groups is the responsibility of the government. The government through its redistributive function is in a position to address the problem, provided that it does not tamper with the market with its natural distributive mechanism, or penalise incentive by imposing too high a rate of taxation to the point of seriously dampening investment and growth.

Moreover, past decades of experiences of welfarism teach us that equalitarian schemes of re-distribution in general bear mixed results, creating in the longer run a culture of dependency on one hand and eroding the moral sense of personal accountability on the other, both being detrimental to the spirit of a civil society.

The above arguments may sound persuasive at first sight but they are not without flaws on closer inspection. Before I proceed to give a fuller picture of how growth under the regime of the market actually subverts equality and how inequality will eventually choke off growth, let me first give a very brief comment on these arguments.

The problem with the first argument and the second one is that they assume the trickle-down effect and the positive-sum game will work smoothly and last indefinitely. By extension, this means that an ever-widening income or wealth disparity of whatever magnitude has little lasting negative impact. This, as I will argue later, is not necessarily the case. Even common sense tells us that such a situation cannot last forever and that these assumptions indicate mere intellectual idleness or escapism. With regard to the marginal productivity theory, the ethicalness embodied in this argument is more apparent than real. It is rooted more in expediency in input–output measurement than in the principle of fairness. Besides, experiences show that in practice, market return to factor input is not the only mode of distribution adopted in all walks of economic life. The fourth argument assumes that the government has the competence, the will and the necessary resources to do the job and do it well. As borne out by recent experiences in many Western nations, this can be very much removed from reality.

How the Rich and Capital Owners Are Empowered

Over time, unfettered economic growth brings about an irreversible outcome of formidable significance. It empowers the rich and capital owner to the eventual state of disrupting the ecology of capitalism with dire consequences. Such empowering is not unexpected, given the fundamental and structural asymmetry between capital and labour and given the fact that the main engines of growth and wealth creation i.e. the modern firm and corporations, that have huge power to dominate the distribution of output are vastly owned and practically controlled by the rich. Whereas capital is storable, accumulative and flexible, labour is not. It is true that capital and labour work hand in hand in producing the kind of economic and technological miracle we witness today. But when the balance of power is chronically tilted towards one party, i.e. capital, by excessively rewarding it, the chemistry of the relationship will change.

The empowering of the rich consists in four dimensions, interacting with and reinforcing one another. The first is the huge leverage that capital can enjoy under the existing institutional framework. The rich and their firms have access to credit in a way that the ordinary folks do not. With capital begetting capital, the modern corporation can enlist vast exterior sources for financing their investment, especially by way of using borrowings and numerous other financial engineering techniques to enhance their overall rate of return. By contrast, the earning ability of labour is, sadly, effort-bound, time-bound and skill-bound.

The second source of power is scale. With access to credit come the advantages of scale both in the realms of the operation of the corporation and personal wealth management. These include increased bargaining power, competitive competence, monopolising advantage and even room for tax evasion. These advantages, in turn, engender access to more credit and other resources. The result is a familiar positive feedback loop. As mentioned before, the multi-tiered and cross-shareholding corporations working in synergy with financiers is a paradigmatic example in playing the game of scale via merger and acquisition.

With the back-up of the above two factors, the rich acquire the third kind of power, namely, rent extracting power, both of the soft and the hard kind (Rent I and Rent II). In many economies, such rent seeking and extracting activities take place in a systematic and massive scale via intense lobbying activities financed and engineered by the capital owners and the firms they control. Needless to say, the return to lobbying and political manipulation in a wide array of areas can be enormous, resulting in an economic landscape further slanting to the already rich. In the realm of taxation, for example, the US super rich, as a result of the convoluted nature of the tax code, actually pay on average a lower tax rate than the less well-off. The average tax rate in 2007 on the top 400 households is only 16.6 percent, considerably lower than the 20.4 percent for taxpayers in general. Also, US corporations pay less than one quarter of all federal income tax while the ordinary folk pay the remaining three-quarters.

Part of the slanting of the economic landscape in favour of capital is, of course, due to the emergence of modern finance and a prosperous financial sector. The impacts consist in several dimensions. First is its ability to dominate the real sector. When joining hands with their financiers, large corporations now with enormous resources in their command enjoy a "predatory" position over many other enterprises in the real sector. The fluidity of financial assets and the "financial technology" in their command enable them to engineer complex corporate structures via mergers, acquisitions, corporate re-shuffling and leveraged buyouts etc. These activities, needless to say, reap huge fortunes for the "financial engineers" and behind them, the capital owners. Interestingly enough, takeover activities spearheaded by financial technology, especially of the hostile kind, do not often lead to more competitive markets or economic efficiency. Many of them benefit enormously the financiers themselves as the firms concerned take on massive debts. As it turns out, many takeovers lead to reduction of employment, raise CEO pay, encourage short-termism but fail to drive productivity.

The second kind of power enjoyed by the financial sector especially in Finance II and Finance III is derived from its rapid rate of expansion, sucking not only financial resources within the financial system, but also resources from the real sector including human talents. Over time the real sector as a whole, while benefiting from the said development in the first stage, gradually loses out with the expanding scale and power of the financial sector. Third, many of the so-called financial innovations are, unlike real innovations that promote our standard of living, designed to facilitate more borrowings and to circumvent regulations, which may lower long run economic performance.

The Rise of the New Extracting Class

The rich, the moneyed class and the firms they control could not by themselves have accomplished that much without a class of "aides" consisting of professionals equipped with sophisticated skills and knowledge in management, marketing, accounting, taxation, finance, strategic planning, law, lobbying and so on. Peter Drucker categorically calls this class "the knowledge workers" with a neutral connotation. He predicts that the world tomorrow will be dominated by the value-creating power of this class of workers who will gradually dwarf that of the blue-collar workers (1964).

Many years on, Drucker's prediction turns out to be only partially correct. Knowledge workers they may be, but a sizeable portion of such knowledge they possess is actually at the service of the capital-owning class in extracting rent from the economy at large. There is, of course, still a large group of knowledge workers working in the real production arena, including engineers, architects, scientists, researchers of different descriptions, medical practitioners, as well as technologists in different fields. But alongside there also emerges another large group of knowledge workers who are engaged in re-distributive and purely extracting activities. The dividing line between the two groups is often blurred, with some members engaging simultaneously in both kinds of activities.

With the gradual diffusion of ownership, modern companies and corporations entrust their management to a class of professionals. John Kenneth Galbraith calls this class the "technostructure" which in practice controls the companies in the industrial system constituting the main production engine of the modern industrial economy (1967). The familiar theme of owner–management relationship and the problem of principal–agent arising from such arrangement have been widely researched. The upshot is that a complicated but "unholy" alliance or partnership between shareholders and their managers emerges, with the management on the ascendency and gradually getting the upper hand.[12] Galbraith argues that the technostructure does not act to maximise profit as that involves the risk of failure, but principally to maintain the organisation. Moreover, the remuneration of these managers is usually tied to performance chiefly in the form of bonus and share options. Because leveraged options on the share price are such a large portion of their compensation, managers run their business not for long-term profit but for short-term return on equity. This is usually done by way of manipulating and boosting equity prices of listed companies, say by buying back shares so shrinking their equity base. This results in a widespread business culture known as the "bonus culture" (Smithers, 2013). The average shareholder, too small to exert influence, also prefers more tangible and short-term return. The ramification for corporate strategy is that long-term real investment tends to be shunned while investment in rent-seeking and manipulative activities which promise more short-term and handsome return is generally preferred.

With the gradual scaling up of big corporations, holding companies and multi-nationals, the resources in command by their CEOs are escalating in huge proportions. Teaming up with their closely affiliated government officials, they form altogether into some kind of "elite network". Since deals among this network can be of mammoth size and involve complicated regulations and rules, mutual trust becomes an increasingly decisive factor. Also since personal time and energy are scarce resources for these top elites, they usually try to confine their key dealings to familiar members within their circle. A new monopolistic "relationship market" thus emerges, with prohibitively high entry threshold and entry cost.

Since relationship and mutual trust govern importantly these deals, mutually acceptable rent extraction by this elite group facilitated by their "accommodative" bureaucrats, becomes an important factor or even a convention in deal closing.[13] Besides, as many of these big deals are investments into the future, present market prices can only act as reference benchmarks, leaving much room for the sharing of the "spoil". Partly because this elite network holds enormous power in allocating societal resources and partly because its members form themselves practically into a highly exclusive, privileged "club", the benefit they can extract is of a tall order. Hence the incredibly high remuneration some of these CEOs receive.[14]

From the value visibility framework, the huge CEO pay is also attributable to the increasingly complex organisation of the modern corporation with its multi-level and cross-holding structures, its wide business interests and its cross-border operations, which altogether render the value of the real contribution of the CEO highly difficult.

To execute the deals thus made, this elite club enlists a supporting group of knowledgeable professionals, particularly in the areas of accounting, law, taxation and financing. A trickling down of rent thus takes place, with the outer circle group to the "club" also receiving a disproportionately high level of remuneration. On the surface, they may be receiving market pay, but actually their compensation packages can be tailor-made to hide significant amounts of rent and to reflect rent differentials. Needless to say, professionals of lesser importance and status also receive, to different extents, benefits partaking the nature of rent. All together, these different "concentric" rings form a rent-collecting party, parasitic on the big deals made by the top elite management circle. They share the "spoil" in accordance with their positions reflecting their value, trustworthiness and dispensability.

The further a knowledge worker is positioned outside the elite club, the more his pay reflects the market price until the point is reached where the less skilful receive a pay governed essentially by a competitive market. Needless to say, this less skilful group constitutes the bulk of the knowledge workforce, including the middle and the junior knowledge workers. Sure there are still significant income differentials among knowledge workers with similar qualifications and experiences, but it is likely that these reflect chiefly inter-sectoral differences in rent collection or monopoly profit generation.

As a result of diminishing value visibility caused by the advance of rent, the modern labour market is undergoing a polarisation process of multiple dimensions. The first level of polarisation results in the formation of a top elite circle or the so-called "0.1–0.5 percent" segment versus the rest of the workforce, with the former taking away the lion's share of societal income and wealth. The second level of polarisation results in an increasingly widening gap between the so-called knowledge workers and the least skilled workers. Within the community of knowledge workers, the gap widens between the rent-related group and the market-oriented group, the former getting decidedly more advantage over the latter. Within this smaller circle of rent-related group of knowledge workers, those who are directly parasitic on the top elite circle, especially in the managing of the latter's wealth and business by applying their legal, financial, accounting and taxation expertise, stand to gain most.

On the surface, upward social mobility on the economic front seems to stay in the industrial world with many success stories to tell, but the overall situation is getting dismal. This is particularly so with respect to the largest group of the workforce, i.e. the mass of the least skilled workers who are gradually marginalised during this process of polarisation.

On the Natural Rate of Unemployment

In the aftermath of the appearance of the Philipps Curve in the 1950s, it was widely held that the rate of unemployment is inversely related to the rate of inflation, When the correlation posited was proven to be of limited validity,[15] a theory of natural rate of unemployment was advanced in its stead (Friedman 1968). The theory posits that if the market is allowed to operate freely, the rate of unemployment will settle at a "natural" rate.

It is generally recognised that, unlike the product market, the labour market is, for various reasons, relatively difficult to clear. Hence unemployment to different degrees, of necessity, exist. For holders of the "natural rate" thesis, such difficulties do not matter. According to them, as long as we discount the frictional and structural factors that cause unemployment, including say, the level of minimum wage, workers' resistance to moving in order to fill job vacancies, the trade unions' capacity to push for raises, unemployment will settle at its "natural rate" in the long run. By implication, they argue that the more intrusive such structural imperfections are, the higher the natural unemployment rate would be. Government monetary and fiscal policies might temporarily lower unemployment below its natural level at the expense of causing higher inflation, but they have no effect on the natural rate in the long run.

Note that when the proponent of the natural rate of unemployment talks about structural factors, he is talking about those that operate at the static market level. Paradoxically, the exact reason for the impossibility of the existence of a natural rate of unemployment is also structural but of a macro and dynamic nature. As a matter of fact, the natural rate theory, albeit camouflaged partly as a dynamic theory by drawing a long run conclusion, is actually founded on a static conception of the economy. The reality is that as an economy develops, it is actually evolving towards a new state. The structure of an economy at a particular point of time can be hugely different from that at another stage in its path of evolution. History shows that the direction of evolution moves generally from a labour-intensive economy to a capital-intensive one; from a product-based economy to a service-based one; from a market dominated economy to a rent dominated economy; and from an economy that relies on simple skills to one that relies on multiple, sophisticated skills etc. These differences would reveal themselves in terms of the changing proportions of the following macro-structural features: high skilled versus low skilled workers; labour-intensive versus capital-intensive industries; the service versus the manufacturing sectors; sunrise versus sunset industries, big enterprises versus SMEs; market versus non-market sectors; market-directed versus rent dominated sectors; homogeneous versus heterogeneous products, etc. As can be expected, the structure of unemployment in these contrasting realms can differ substantially, with varying ramifications for the wage-determining process which in turn affect the level of employment. As a result, there is no reason to expect the composition of an economy at different stages of development to be similar and for that matter, the same for the respective unemployment rates of these different stages.

With these structural and compositional differences, it is not surprising that in the course of evolution of an economy, factors other than market forces, say history, social custom and convention, government action, unionisation, cross-border wage level or parity consideration within the corporation also come to play some role in wage determination. Given that cross-sectoral mobility of labour cannot always be perfect because of differences in skill-set requirements, and given that some sectors must be lagging behind in their development or becoming obsolete, the wage level and wage structure of certain sectors would take time to adjust in line with the lead sectors and tend to be sticky for some prolonged period, with workers who find it hard to adapt remaining as wage-takers and wage-followers rather than becoming active agents in wage-setting. This being the case, it is obvious that wage determination which affects importantly the level of unemployment is a highly complex process governed not only by micro-economic forces (for example the value of marginal product of labour in the standard doctrine), but also by changes in macro-structural factors.

From the above, it follows that the rates of unemployment in different stages of development of an economy or across different economies can differ widely. Alternatively put, as an economy evolves and experiences changes in its sectoral composition with ramifications for the wage-determining process, it is quite unlikely that there exists one and only one set of natural rate of unemployment. By extension, if a theory were to posit that there exist multiple sets of natural rates of unemployment with respect to different types of economies or to different stages of development of an economy, it then loses its explanatory value and becomes nothing more than an over-generalised hypothesis devoid of empirical content. In other words, while we can still say that there exists a natural rate of unemployment from a static perspective, there is no meaningful natural rate of unemployment from a dynamic view unless we can track down the frictional and structural factors for each and every one of such scenarios in the developmental pathway.

Marginalisation of the Less Skilled and the Less Resourceful

At odds with the idea that an economy settles with a long-run natural rate of unemployment, we discern in recent decades a disturbing trend of chronically deteriorating employment across the industrial world. As can be expected, this goes hand in hand with another similarly worrying trend, namely, an increasing distributive disparity of income. In the previous section, I have analysed the rise of the extracting class as one plausible explanation. In the standard economic literature, unemployment leading to worsening income disparity is often attributed to three major causes.

One cause is technological progress and its economic consequence of "robot-sourcing". Technological development brings about skill-biased technical change which enhances the productivity of highly skilled workers while auto-mating the jobs of the less skilled. Over the past forty years, the cost of investment goods relative to consumption goods has declined roughly by 25 percent.[16] This results in a conspicuous displacement of low-skilled labour as well as junior and middle-level management. Another cause is globalisa-tion or "off-shore sourcing", transferring massive jobs from the industrial world to the emerging nations. Yet another one is the gradual liberalisation and de-unionisation of the labour market, with many jobs changing to work contracts or part-time and temporary engagements. At the same time, labour unions are losing their bargaining power and are therefore of diminished help to counter the above development. With regard to technological pro-gress, there are two dimensions to technology as a growth driver, the universal and the contingent. The contingent side consists of two aspects. First, there is always uncertainty and unpredictability as to the content, intensity and timing of technological development. Thus in a special sense, the neoclassical growth economist is not too incorrect in treating technology as an exogenous factor. Second, there can be huge differentials with respect to the growth and employment effects among different clusters of technology. There exist cases where technology can help drive growth but not employment or can even depress employment. In this regard, the advance of the modern digital techno-logy also commonly labelled as information and communication technology (ICT) is particularly disturbing. From the stance of capitalists, displacement of labour by automation is a fundamental business strategy to stay in a competitive market. It is just that in the past history of capitalist develop-ment, the positive employment effects of growth have managed to more than offset the negative impacts. But with the advent of ICT, the employment effect is radically changed. What with the reduction of "secondary employment", say in the realm of replacement work, the "dematerialisation" of economic activity, and the distributive consequence of the "winner-takes-all", the digital revolution leading to a "digital food chain" (Galbraith, 2014) is opening up a great divide between a relatively skilled and wealthy group and the rest of society.

What is, however, less appreciated is that growing unemployment among the less skilled reflects also the inevitable result of structural changes brought about by the subversive effects of economic growth itself. Apart from the above standard explanation, there are several additional factors brought about by economic growth that crucially impact employment and distributive disparity.

Just as technological progress affects negatively the employment of low skilled labour, progress in management thinking and techniques that accompany economic progress also contributes negatively to the employment of this class. To maximise value for a firm or its shareholders, the management of a company needs continually to keep operating cost under good control, especially during periods of economic downturn or intense competition. Given the multi-faceted and complex relationships between labour and management in a firm,[17] labour management is never an easy job. Building a highly motivated but smaller team of workforce is clearly a preferable human resources strategy. This strategy is now getting easier to implement with the formidable information systems now available. For example, credit ratings of job candidates can now be easily obtained and become more widely adopted. In the same vein, mistakes and mediocrity are becoming more difficult to hide.[18] This, together with the strategy of adopting a cost-effective technology that matches its specific human resources policy, constitutes the philosophy of "lean management" (in the broad sense) which becomes widely popular in the business world.

The "financialisation" of the modern corporation with its increased orientation towards adding shareholding value via financial engineering plays no small role in encouraging lean management. "Financialisation" making use of the so-called "financial technology" is highly knowledge-intensive and does not benefit mass employment. It may be argued that the increased financial resources of a corporation may uplift its appetite for additional investment and hence employment, but it is also possible that the enhanced financial resources are used for further financialisation via projects like mergers and acquisitions without actually benefiting labour employment, if not diminishing it.

As an economy makes progress, specialisation of skills goes hand in hand. Specialisation spurs growth chiefly through value creation by innovation and enhanced productivity. With the creation of more and more market niches, knowledge workers naturally form themselves into sub-groups of "professional guilds" with growing monopolistic power. Within these groups, workers developing their individuated modes of value creation and innovation have less and less in common with one another. Collective bargaining on a large scale and on a united front is no longer valued. This weakens the need for unionisation.

Rent seeking as a result of growth also leads to less demand for collective action among the highly skilled workers. Since by nature, rent seeking is done discreetly, workers striving for rent or benefitting from rent-seeking activities have less need to form open coalitions for collective bargaining, which could then expose their hidden agenda. This, too, renders unionisation and collective bargaining less relevant. Furthermore, with rent trickling down from the top elite circle to a widening circle and as the former commands more and more power and resources, the less skilled group down at the bottom of the organisation ladder is further enfeebled in their bargaining power. As of today, fewer than 7 percent of private-sector workers are unionised in the United States.

In summary, the by-products of economic progress, namely, advances in technology resulting in the reduction of the price of capital goods, the advent of lean management leading to more efficient modes of business organisation and less demand for low-skilled labour, the financialisation of the modern corporation, as well as specialisation and innovation, which together with the prevalence of rent-extracting activities, weaken the power of labour with negative impact on both employment and real wage growth over time.

The above developments should not come as a surprise. Increasing income disparity caused by a higher rate of unemployment or slower growth of real wage or a combination of both reflects multi-dimensionally the increasing power of capital. As an economy progresses the balance is tilted further and further against labour in general and the less skilled in particular. Needless to say, unfettered economic growth without taking good care of its negative consequences can be potentially hazardous to society. In light of its subversive potential, economic growth cannot be the sole objective of an economy.

How the Financial Cycle Hurts the Financially Less Resourceful

As if an increasing rate of unemployment and sluggish wage rate growth are not enough, economic growth further wreaks havoc on the less resourceful group (which generally overlaps with the less skilful group) via the financial cycles it generates. As economic growth propels the financial sector and spurs the "financialisation" of an economy, financial crises also grow in magnitude. And, sad to say, a financial collapse harms the less resourceful in a disproportionate manner because of its differential wealth destroying effects, with the less resourceful often bearing the brunt of the impact.

The first reason is that the less resourceful group including say, the lower middle and lower middle class are generally investment-illiterate, even if they have the spare savings for investment. As a financial cycle advances and the speculative atmosphere heats up, they are gradually lured into the game, first with prudence and suspicion, until newly gained profits convince them that this would be a once-in-a-life opportunity to make a fortune. Eventually some of them take part in the more volatile investments, for example options and derivatives, or in the highly leveraged commodity and Forex markets.

The sad thing is that since they are generally investment-illiterate and since they enter the market at a more "mature" and hence more speculative stage, the average cost of their investment portfolios is higher than that of the veteran rich, who have always stayed in the game. In the course of their participation, as they go through smaller market fluctuations and begin to pick up confidence through making a bit of profit in the upward rising phase of the financial cycle, they become gradually emboldened and start to throw "good" money into the game either from the little savings they have or through borrowings. Though they may make initial gain from their earlier deals, their subsequent investments are often acquired at rising asset prices. This means that as they continue to make new investments, they are buying at an increasingly higher and eventually "bubble" prices. Moreover, their scant asset bases even after borrowing are generally too small to diversify risk. Worse still, this group of small investors is neither sensitive enough nor psychologically prepared to exit before or when the bubble bursts. And when the day of reckoning comes with it massive wealth-destroying effect, it is usually this group that registers the biggest loss relative to the size of their original asset base.

Not only that. Apart from the loss of wealth and the borrowings that have to be paid off (unless they declare bankrupt), this group often faces double hardship in the post-crash period, the more so in the case of the recent 2007–8 collapse. Yes, the economy, say in the US eventually picks up, but for a long-stretched period, the recovery is pale and largely of a jobless kind. In this regard, one can note another asymmetry between the economic power of the firm and that of the individual worker. The former, in command of more resources including access to credit in the capital market, as well as professional and managerial resources, can take initiative to meet the challenge and more likely to recover faster. On the other hand, the ordinary folk are in a relatively passive and pitiful mode. Little wonder that since the recovery in the US began after the "Great Recession", 90 percent of the income gains have accrued to 10 percent of the population. And in the event the post-crash period happens to degenerate into a deflation trap, the burden of debt borne by this group is even more frightening. Should this trend continue into the future, we can expect the rate of unemployment to deteriorate with each new round of financial collapse in the future (apart from being caused by technological and globalisation factors).

In previous epochs, the less privileged groups may look to their generally generous government for help. Perhaps not any more. In the aftermath of post-2007–8, many governments in the industrial world are already highly debt-ridden. Some governments have spent relentlessly to save their precarious financial sectors and their too-big-to-fail banks, while some others feel compelled to adopt austerity measures to get out of their fiscal plight. None of these are good news for the less resourceful group in the present-day economies.

Summary

Economic inequality is jointly caused by two sets of factors, one structural and the other dynamic. Structurally, there is a big asymmetry between capital and labour both productivity-wise and income-wise. Dynamically, economic growth results in the structural factors being deepened and worsened over time. Generally speaking, inequality is caused by the rich getting more powerful and influential and conversely by the mass being impoverished. The latter process comes about by way of a higher rate of unemployment or of stagnation in wage rate growth or as a result of cyclical financial crisis, which in turn are caused by factors such as technological progress, globalisation, the financialisation of the economy etc. Some other arguments have also been put forward to explain the rising inequality. For example, rising divorced rates result in more single parents, which affect the quality of education received by their offspring, as well as increases in property prices in recent decades world-wide especially in the most desirable cities, leading to a more polarised wealth distribution among the haves and have-nots. Most of the structural factors have been extensively dealt with by different schools in the existing economic literature and what I have done in the foregoing analysis is merely to supplement or to highlight some of these views.

What needs to be emphasised is that the ultimate factor generally ignored is the dynamics of growth under the present capitalist institutional regime. Growth for whatever reason it is caused, is generally seen to be a benign factor, essential to the well-being of the economy at large and the less resourceful as well. Thus the causal link between growth and inequality is easily missed because the benefits of growth come far earlier and, being tangible, are cognitively far more conspicuous than its ills. Given the cognitive opacity of this relationship, it is hardly surprising that there is no established systematic relationship between income gaps and financial crisis. This is another grand economic illusion, but one that is seldom taken seriously.

In Chapter 1 I argue that growth is possible in an economy when both risk and value are readily ascertainable. The irony is that as growth surges ahead, it creates, even as the basic institutional regime remains unchanged, an economic environment that is no longer conducive to the visibility of risk and value. Economic growth leads to and results from the proliferation of multiple "market forms" and "corporate forms" with varying degrees of value visibility. While prices in the resultant market forms are still perceived by market participants to stand objectively for value, they are in reality not necessarily so. In many markets, prices that are apparently seen to represent exchange values are getting increasingly divorced from their real or fundamental values. One consequence of diminished value visibility as well as the collective misperceptions arising, is that risk, too, becomes less visible and ascertainable, regardless of whether or not the market participants themselves are aware of such changes. Moreover, decreasing risk and value ascertainability, as I have argued, create the very conditions leading on the one hand to financial instability and on the other hand to deteriorating distributive disparity which slows down growth, particularly if it translates into less equality of opportunity for the next generation. Moreover it is becoming quite obvious that high levels of poverty can stifle investment and innovation. All these impact negatively on economic equality in a vicious circle.

In Chapter 1 I point out that the Solow residual can be interpreted either from the stance of causal explanation or from that of factor receipt accounting. I argue that we should start off with the latter because an understanding of the basic ingredients of the residual from the accounting point of view is more fundamental. With the discussions behind us, I now venture to offer some preliminary guesswork. My guess is that part of the factor receipt residual may have gone to the financial sector. Consider the extraordinary rise of say, the US financial sector, which requires little capital physical stock for production, rises from 11 to 12 percent of GNP back in the 1980s to 20 to 21 percent. During the same period, manufacturing which makes extensive use of capital stock has slipped from about 25 percent to just 12 percent.

Consider another possibility. The phenomenal rise of big corporations and their "financialisation" and rent-seeking activities have resulted in big profit, much of which stays within the corporation as retained profit, or as reserve for further leveraged financialisation activities, or as dividend going into the hands of the shareholders (capital owners). For example, distributed profit as a share of US corporate profit used to stand at 35 to 45 percent but was 60 percent since the late 1970s. Such receipts are not fully reflected in the respective receipts of labour and capital and they probably constitute an important portion of the Solow residual. In the same vein, from the viewpoint of causal factor explanation, the rise of rent-seeking and re-distributive activities that go along with the expansion of corporations means that the growth of GDP must reflect not merely the overall productivity of labour and capital, (i.e. total factor productivity) but also the former types of activities. That is to say, an important component of the causal factor for the residual might well be rent-seeking, apart from institutional factors that make the utilisation of capital land labour more efficient (as captured in the notion of total factor productivity).

Notes

1 The defining feature of wealth under the regime of capitalism is the propensity to re-invest.
2 This does not mean that fixed income financial products are free of risk. As opposed to government bonds which are generally safe, e.g. US Treasury Bonds, some high-yield fixed income instruments, e.g. corporate bonds, are liable to default.
3 It is interesting to note that unlike in the goods market, an abundant supply of financial products does not necessarily depress asset price as long as an additional supply of liquidity offsets any downward tendency or when investors have positive expectations of price movements. It is likely in such circumstances investors take the cue from rising asset prices that they will go up further, thereby they will be induced to hold on to their assets or increase their holdings.
4 While their origins date back centuries, modern financial derivatives came into their own in the late 1980s and early 1990s.
5 In its weak version. See Chapter 3.
6 The issue of instability is not new. It can be dated back to the days of John Stuart Mill, Alfred Marshall, Knut Wicksell and Irving Fisher. Conventional analysis on the question of instability usually focuses on several structural features. The first one is the basic mismatch between the bank's short-term deposits and its loans

which generally extend beyond the short-term. The second is the excess debt that goes to the purchase of existing assets rather than to real capital investment, with the result that asset prices traded do not necessarily stay in line with economic fundamentals. The third is the excess credit creation made possible by the lack of limit put on leveraging. Still there are scholars who attribute financial instability to the incoherent policies of central bankers, particularly when the latter are inclined to treat credit contraction and expansion in an asymmetric manner. While each of the above arguments largely holds, they do not add up to a coherent theory nor do they provide a dynamic theory of instability generation.

Scholars who argue for the inherent instability of the financial system in general offer three main types of explanation. The first focuses on the less-than-rational features of human decision-making, for example, crowd psychology and herd instinct. The second focuses on the inherent imperfections of information in a market, namely the amount of market completion and the level of transparency that exist. Third, the future is characterised by inherently irreducible uncertainty and not mathematically modelable risk. A coherent account is given by Hyman Minsky. His Instability Hypothesis posits that instability originates in the very financial institutions that make capitalism possible. Financial markets can generate their own internal forces, which cause waves of credit expansion and asset inflation followed by waves of credit contraction and asset deflation. The chief destabilising force is debt, the accumulation, distribution and valuation of which result in some kind of dynamic that injects uncertainty into the financial system. When the amount of unserviceable debt balloons to a certain level, the system collapses (1982).

In this book, I distinguish three contributing factors. The first is the nature of institutional design (permitting leverage and credit that weaken household financial budget constraint acting as an equilibrating force). The second is the absence of an independent reality check such as the act of actual consumption in the goods market, with the result that asset values are monolithically believed to be fully reflected by market prices. The third is the failure of risk management due to the cognitive asymmetry between Risk I and Risk II. All together these three factors constitute an institutional-cognitive framework. The dynamic disequilibrium of the financial system is driven by the interactions between the leverage institution with the cognitive shortcoming of the investor. It is therefore not uncertainty per se that acts as a de-stabilising force, but that investors, handicapped by their valuation tools, come under the illusion that they are able to ascertain risk whereas actually they fail to do so, especially in the later part of a financial cycle.

Contrary perhaps to common sense, increasing inequality may well be another cause of financial stability. With increasing affluence, the conspicuous consumption of the higher income group gradually induces the rest of society to partake some of the former's behaviours. But because of limited means, they have to resort to excessive borrowings, hence the vast build-up of private debt and consumer credit.

7 The history of finance shows a broadly interesting pattern, with new regulations responding to each crisis by increasingly protecting finance more. Five disasters, from 1792 to 1929, together can well explain the origin of the modern financial system.

8 Scholars, however, hold controversial views on how far the repeal of the Act contributes to the 2007–8 crash. Some argue that the boundary between commercial banking and investment banking has largely been eroded long before the repeal.

9 Kevin Phillips, for example, coins the term "Financial Mercantilism" to convey the idea that the new financial sector is closely interconnected with government politics and power and that the US government and business collaborate to suspend or stymie market forces (2008).

10 Since the 2007–8 crash, many solutions have been offered. Broadly speaking these come under five headings: (1) Fix the too-big-to-fail problem; (2) Limit the leverage; (3) Expose "weapons of mass financial destruction"; (4) Bring shadow banking

into the light; (5) Reboot the culture of finance. Broadly speaking there are two schools of thought. One is the micro-structural school which assumes that the problems are essentially those of market imperfections, opacity and perverse incentives. The core policy is to tackle the too-big-to-fail problem by way of imposing losses on debt holders, meaning we need to smoothly turn debt claims into equity claims when necessary. The second, called the macro-Minsky school, argues that the drivers of instability are deeper than those amenable to increased transparency and the reform of incentives. Reform-wise, it recommends focusing on macroprudential oversight and policy response, in particular monitoring aggregate leverage and aggregate maturity transformation (Turner, 2012).

11 At his speech at Osawatomie in 2011 (*The Economist*, 13 October 2012, p. 28).

12 Recent events indicate that a wave of shareholder activism is on the increase, with a fraction of discontented shareholders seeking to capture some power from the management, e.g. over pay structure. This development may result in bringing back some checks and balances but the overall dominance of the management over owners can hardly be challenged.

13 A recent survey shows that around two-thirds of people in the US thought that their governments were run in the service of "big interests" compared with the remaining who thought otherwise.

14 Another reason is that CEO remunerations, however high they may be, do not seem to be exorbitant when spread over a large number of shareholdings, especially when dividend paid out to the individual shareholder looks reasonable.

15 Modern versions distinguish between short-run and long-run effects on unemployment. The "short-run Phillips Curve" is also called the expectation-argumented Phillips Curve because it shifts up when inflationary expectations rise. While there is a short run trade-off between unemployment and inflation, it has not been observed in the long run. The "long run Phillip Curve" is also identified as the natural rate of unemployment or "NAIRU".

16 *The Economist*, 2 November 2013.

17 It is widely recognised that the labour market is quite unique, or at least structurally very different from the commodity or the product market, in that labour markets are more difficult to clear. Numerous researches have been conducted in this regard. In the following I put forward some views from the price–value analytics that I develop in this book. In the product market, the matching of buyers and sellers is relatively simple. Although suppliers have to adjust themselves to a wide array of varying and changing buyer preferences in due course, the actual matching process at the front stage is of a simple, one-way character. The buyer himself makes a choice from a given set of market options that he encounters. But in the employment market, the matching is a two-way one. At the time a worker mediates on a job opening and appraises its appropriateness for himself, the employing firm is doing something similar. Besides, there is another intriguing difference. In the product market, the buyer generally finds it easy to judge and compare the triangular relationship between price, expected value and realised value in his act of purchase and consumption. The gaps that may emerge among these variables stand out quite clearly in his mind. The supplier, on the other hand, would find it far more difficult to read such gaps. He can infer consumer satisfaction only indirectly from the sales performance after a certain period or statistically from consumer surveys he conducts. A kind of cognitive veil thus insulates one party from the other. In the case of the labour market the perceptions held by the employer and employee are more often of a complex, interactive and dynamic nature. This is particularly the case for jobs where the skill-sets required are multiple and complicated and where the value of the marginal product of the individual worker cannot be easily ascertained, especially if he works as part of a team.

For the employee whose job requires a relatively complex skill-set, the mismatch between the remuneration he receives and the overall expected value he derives from his job may be quite substantial due to a multiplicity of factors (including the working environment, promotion opportunities, room for learning, variance between the job description and the actual duties required etc.). From the employer's point of view, he may also find his employee falling short of his expectation from different angles, (for example his actual performance, his work attitude and ethic, his socialising and team work skills, his ability to adapt to the culture of the company, etc.). The co-existence and possible interactions of these multiple perceptional gaps means that both parties tend to be more prudent in the management of their relationship, with respect to areas like job search, work contract, performance appraisal, dismissal, resignation etc. These features explain in part the complexity of the nature of employment and why the labour market cannot be easily cleared, especially for jobs where multiple skills are essential.

18 Ironically, this applies mainly to the middle and junior levels of management. The contrary actually happens as rent-seeking activities act as a veil to cover up real values.

Part II
Solution

3 The Vain Search for Solution

3.1 The Market as a Non-solution for Inequality

The Consequences of Economic Inequality

There is little need to repeat in detail the effects of economic inequality. High and persistent unemployment, both the cause and effect as well as manifestation of inequality can have, for example, devastating effects on society beyond the economic sphere. Unemployment erodes self-esteem at the individual level and promotes dislocation, unrest and conflict at the society level. Studies on the co-relation between high rates of health, social problems (obesity, mental illness, homicides, drug abuse, etc.), lower rates of social good (life expectancy, educational performance, trust among strangers, status of women, social mobility, etc.), and heightening inequality abound. All these point unmistakenly to the negative impact of economic inequality on both individual well-being and social cohesion, with dire socio-political consequences.

Within the economic sphere, one serious consequence of high rates of unemployment is the destructive impact on social and human capital. Human skills that are hard-earned but not put to use will be eroded. This is more so in the case of youth unemployment. Apart from imposing an additional burden on social welfare, a high level of unemployment among the young implies a huge loss of potential human capital that an economy needs to build its future and foster growth. Deprived of employment opportunities, the psyche and attitude of this group of well-educated youths on which the future of an economy so critically depends may be irreversibly impaired. In view of these negative elements, any society that aspires seriously to look after the well-being of its individuals and manage properly its internal harmony needs to tackle the problems of economic growth and economic equality at once and in a well-balanced manner. In this chapter, I will examine the conventional solutions and argue why they are not good enough.

The Power and Alleged Supremacy of the Market

The Logic of the Market

The Smithian metaphor of the invisible hand captures neatly the "magic" of the market through the working of the price mechanism. Price signals in a free market enable buyers and sellers to adjust and match their respective preferences, plans and decisions accordingly. As a result, this micro-level adjustment mechanism brings about the greatest efficiency in the allocation of resources economy-wide.

Not only is the market mechanism believed to achieve allocative efficiency of resources for an economy, but it is also alleged to achieve distributive equity in the sense of paying each factor input the value of its marginal product, according to the theory of marginal productivity.

By this logic, the market is seen to be an institution that solves simultaneously the two most important problems in the operation of an economy, namely, allocative efficiency and distributive equity. It thus resolves, elegantly and without deliberate human intervention, tensions that exist between individual interest and collective interest. Private "vice" can therefore lead to public good, as Adam Smith so wisely proclaims.[1] Note, however, that under the individuated order characterising the modern society where private interest is the ruling norm of the day, the term "private vice" is no longer an appropriate description of self-interest.

Wholesale Idealisation and "Ideologisation"

Carried away by the beauty of the idea, the concept of the market becomes subsequently idealised and even mystified. The development takes on two pathways, namely, idealisation at the level of academic enquiry and "ideologisation" at the level of policy-making.

In the realm of idealisation, four different approaches can be identified. If the market looks like a self-equilibrating process, it follows that it will somehow reach a state of equilibrium. The interesting academic question arising therefore is whether or not the alleged equilibrium is guaranteed to exist and whether and under what conditions that equilibrium is unique, determinable and stable. A huge technical literature addressing these issues under the label general equilibrium theory (GE) subsequently emerges. The point to note is that the proof of the existence of a unique and stable equilibrium requires the making of a number of most extraordinary and unrealistic assumptions, including perfect rationality of the individual, complete information about all prices both now and in the future, and the conditions necessary for perfect competition. The method of proof employed is again one of reverse engineering, i.e. working backward to choose which assumption is required or can be relaxed.

GE theorists do not defend their assumptions of perfect markets, etc. on the ground that markets are actually perfect. Rather, they hope to build an idealised invisible hand model that would provide an arch framework for building more realistic models incorporating observable "imperfections", such as monopolies, trade unions, protectionism, etc. However, it is one thing to make these "perfection" assumptions and quite another to "reverse-engineer" them in order to model imperfections. There is, furthermore, no reason why we should not deal directly with these so-called "imperfect" phenomena.

In response to the criticism that the GE theory is static in character, a new generation of GE theory under the label dynamic stochastic general equilibrium (DSGE) models emerges, picturing an economy as moving frame-by-frame over time, hit occasionally by stochastic or random shocks (technological, fiscal, monetary, etc.). But its assumption that the core economy restores instantaneously back to its unique equilibrium retains the very fundamental feature of the GE theory.

The GE theory and its descendant DSGE are in substance built on a "mathematical metaphor", with the unintended consequence of ushering economic theorising back into the realm of metaphysics instead of advancing toward a genuine scientific discipline. The sophisticated mathematics used is nothing more than some kind of "reverse metaphor" which goes in the opposite direction, namely, using a more complicated one to explain a simpler fact.

Similarly the "spontaneous order" theory of the market employs a physical–chemical metaphor, rooted in the idea of the equilibrating force in nature. The spread of the idea of the spontaneous order in economics (also called the "extended order" or "catallaxy" by Hayek) goes with the idea that self-interested human agents in a world of decentralised information make the best use of available information and their knowledge, thus leading to the most desirable social outcomes (which, strictly speaking, is not very much different from the Smithian metaphor of the invisible hand). While the original idea of information and knowledge dispersion makes good sense, further extension of the idea lapses into an idealism of "self-organisation". In the extreme form, it posits that the market, driven by human instinct and self-interest and left alone, would spontaneously achieve maximal good for everyone without any external support or intervention. But the truth is that the success of the market as an institution depends critically on the right kind of rules and regulations laid down by the state as well as on certain social customs and conventions evolving congenially over time. Both sets of factors contribute importantly to raising the level of risk and value ascertainability of market transactions, thus enabling the market to function smoothly. Admittedly, the appearance of spontaneity in a mature and well-functioning market is undeniable, but the idea itself is still nothing more than a metaphorical construction, especially when we consider the fact that markets do fail and market failures of different types are not uncommon.

Karl Polanyi, in his *The Great Transformation* points out that markets and society are seamlessly bound together. In order for markets to work, society needs to license the turning of things into commodities that can be exchanged in society. Thus in his view, the "self-regulating" market turns out to need society far more than it pretends to (1946).

The third mode of idealisation is manifest in the highly influential hypothesis of rational expectations (originally proposed by John Muth and later becomes popular when used by Robert Lucas, Jr). The hypothesis posits that people do not make systematic errors when predicting the future. Their expectations may be wrong but are correct on average over time. Deviations from their "perfect foresight" are only random. In other words, people's expectations equal true statistical expected values (of economically relevant variables). Since at any specific time a market or the economy has only one equilibrium, people form their expectations around this unique equilibrium. Outcomes that are being forecast do not differ systematically from the market equilibrium results. The fundamental reason why this is the case is that individuals are rational beings who take all available information into account in forming expectations. As a consequence, economic policies that deviate from agents' expectations cannot have lasting effects.

This hypothesis amounts in effect to idealising the cognitive capability of the economic agent, i.e. the agent as a cognitive being cannot be systematically wrong in his prediction of future markets or economic values. It concedes that deviations may occur, but they are random events by nature and are the results of "information shock". Even more esoteric, it assumes that economic agents are capable of seeing the unique market equilibrium and form their expectations around it. These extreme assumptions may be convenient and useful for economic modelling, but they are clearly very much removed from reality. Economic agents may be rational in intention, i.e. in deliberating plans to advance their self-interests. Their expectations may well be reasonable and sensible. But given their cognitive biases and failings (some of them are of a systematic kind), there is no guarantee that the outcomes are correct or that there are no systematic errors between participants' forecasts and what comes to pass, even given the opportunity to correct mistakes. Besides, it is almost common sense that actions among individuals do not always add up to rational outcomes at the macro or aggregate level.[2] As such, expectations of people can be systematically wrong and their errors can be internally generated.

The fourth form of idealisation, under the notion of "Efficient Market Hypothesis (EMH)" is more specific to the financial market, where an enormous amount of information is continually being manufactured and circulated, involving and affecting myriads of decisions by investors. The hypothesis posits that financial market prices unfailingly reflect all past publicly available or even "hidden" information and that the decisions made by investors have actually considered all such information. As in the case of the rational expectations hypothesis, markets are assumed to tend towards equilibrium. Deviations occur in a random fashion and can be attributed to exogenous shocks.

There are three versions of the hypothesis, the "weak", the "semi-strong" and the "strong". The weak version posits that prices on traded assets (e.g. stock, bonds or properties) reflect all past publicly available information. The semi-strong version claims that prices reflect all past publicly available information and those prices instantly change to reflect new public information. The strong version additionally claims that prices instantly reflect even hidden or "insider" information.

Whichever version one holds, the hypothesis is subject to important criticisms. First the assumption that the existence of market prices must imply that the market is informationally efficient or that the traded prices reflect the

rational deliberations and decisions of the investors using all available information, or that no one can out-strategise the market are clearly over-stretched.
Results of empirical studies conducted are mixed and are not entirely consistent
with the hypothesis. Some studies show that stocks with low price-earning
ratios outperform other stocks and yield returns in excess of average market
returns on a risk-adjusted basis. Behavioural economists challenge the
hypothesis from the cognitive perspective by arguing that financial markets
can be inefficient given human cognitive failings.

But the behaviourist challenge, albeit quite popular, is not altogether persuasive and conclusive. Recall that traded prices are the results of the deliberation of
market participants. The behavioural economist might argue that since these
deliberations are subjective interpretations, they are subject to different types
of cognitive pitfalls, such as over-confidence, over-reaction, representative
bias, and various other failings in reasoning and information processing. But
the fallibility of judgment at the individual level can still be irrelevant to the
overall efficiency of the financial market. Quite the contrary, a market allowing
room for mistake correction and plan adjustment can be considered a positive
factor contributing to its efficient functioning. Indeed, the more efficient a
market is, the more likely its investors are able to learn from their mistakes
and adjust their plans accordingly. That is, an efficient market can in principle
efficiently correct the mistakes of the participants. If this were the case, it
speaks for rather than refutes the hypothesis.

Granted that the market is generally efficient, does it also mean that the
market as a whole is always right in the sense of reflecting real value? Yes, the
financial market can be informationally efficient or even ultra-efficient in terms
of mistake correction. Its products can be almost instantly manufactured both
to create and to meet demand. Trading and information transmission can
take place instantaneously without the obstruction of physical distance. But
the existence of these apparently "superior" attributes does not imply the
market is always right in the macro-sense. Recall the "regime shift" towards
leveraged capital gain that takes place in the later stage of development of a
financial cycle when the market grows so volatile that values becomes "pseudo-
ascertainable" (i.e. having merely the appearance of ascertainability), and
when prices are driven more by liquidity expansion than by increases in the
"real" value of the products in line with economic reality. In fact, at the final
stage, when the market becomes "super-efficient" on a massive scale, and when
the momentum of Risk II gathers force, the market is already heading towards
collapse. In other words, we are running into a paradoxical situation where
market efficiency which is a seeming virtue, actually blinds us from deciphering
the "vice" behind. We may perhaps call this the "paradox of efficiency of the
financial market".

The interesting question is why the EMH, the flaws of which are quite
obvious, is widely received both in the academic and the financial circle.[3] For
one thing it does command the virtues of theoretical simplicity and unity. But
it is also probable that upholders of the hypothesis are too intellectually

complacent. Instead of exploring the idiosyncrasies of the financial market, they merely map the characteristics of the perfectly homogeneous goods market together with the notion of general equilibrium onto the financial market and then develop and defend their "metaphor" on sophisticated models and mathematics. For if the goods market should operate efficiently without giving rise to problems, so they ask, why shouldn't the financial market? But alas, they forget that the reality checks that are available in the goods market are seriously lacking in the financial market, resulting in possibilities of mispricing of the real values of their products in a staggering order.

From the angle of risk, the EMH, being basically a static conception, is not well positioned to consider seriously the risk dynamics of a financial market propelled by leverage and its liquidity generating property. Even granted that the hypothesis holds from a cross-sectional analysis, or at the level of individual stock, it is still seriously flawed in that it fails to take into account different types and levels of risk and their dynamics, and that market asset prices may no longer reflect risks at the later stage of the financial cycle. By assuming away especially risk of the systemic kind, it fails to see the growing hazard of Risk II. In other words, its fundamental flaw lies in its equating informational efficiency and spontaneity with risk and value ascertainability.

Instead of seeing the freewheeling financial market as a source of instability, policymakers heed the advice of the EMH and see the financial market as a prototype of the efficient market. The policy implication is, of course, more financial de-regulation and liberalisation, meaning that any obstruction in the way of the free functioning of the financial markets should be removed or reduced to minimum. Without much exaggeration, one can even say that the EMH has become "the working ideology of financial capitalism".

As a summary, it is interesting to note that the four modes of market idealisation capture almost all the essential components of the market. The GE theory idealises on the end-point or the ultimate state of equilibrium and explores the necessary conditions for its existence. The spontaneous order theory idealises on the equilibrating market process. The rational expectations theory idealises on the cognitive capability of the economic agent by positing "perfect foresight", while the EMH idealises the informational spontaneity of the market. Each of them may pose interesting and challenging academic questions. But they are not very useful in throwing light on unearthing the complex reality of the market, let alone the fact that they may actually be posing stumbling blocks on our understanding of its true nature.

While the above four approaches represent fiction-like idealisations in the academic sphere, the faith in the power and supremacy of the market in the policy-making arena takes another turn and develop into some kind of "religious" doctrine, commonly known as "market fundamentalism". The doctrine preaches the natural supremacy of the market and discredits any form of discreet intervention from the government. One reason it gives for rejecting discreet intervention is that even good intentions may bring about unintended consequences that defeat the original purpose. Drawing support from the researches of the public choice school, it argues not only that bureaucrats act out of their self-interest and hidden agenda, but also that very often, the government, lacking comprehensive or relevant knowledge, makes decisions that turn out to be positively harmful.

The problems with market fundamentalism are twofold. The first is the extreme stance it takes. No person in his normal senses would doubt the power of the market, but it would be too much to deny the contribution of rules and regulations needed to support the "natural" functioning of the market and to make up for the latter's deficiency. In practice, markets never function in a vacuum, but instead in a setting of regulations and real-life restrictions which include, say, the location of sales outlets, the qualification of participants, licensing, product liability, failure in delivery, loan default, immigration control, just to name a few. Some of these may, of course, obstruct the market from functioning smoothly. But the market fundamentalist, in his zeal to preserve the purity or the "legendary" natural order of the market, blames whatever shortcomings of the market on government intervention. This is not consistent with empirical evidence.

The second difficulty with the market fundamentalists is that they cannot agree among themselves on how much government they tolerate. Some at the extreme end, i.e. those belonging to the libertarian strand, want as little government as they can possibly conceive of (e.g. Nozick, 1974). Others such as Hayek and Friedman accept that the government does have some indispensable roles. Although they cry out for minimal government, they do not seriously draw a clear line on how much government we should accept. And when they do cite examples of acceptable government roles, they do not provide a theoretical framework to support how the line should be drawn. Hayek, for example, warns us that central planning, giving too much discreet and arbitrary power to the government, may lead irrevocably and eventually to the totalitarian state. On the other hand, although he approves quite a number of piecemeal regulations, he has not systematically made clear the range of "tolerable government", especially in what way and how far government might make up for market inadequacy. Nor has he offered a comprehensive framework to justify the limits of tolerance.[4] All in all, the market fundamentalists themselves cannot make up their mind as to how much room they should leave for government or what exactly they mean by minimal government or at which point the cost of intervention outweighs the benefit. As a result, the positions taken by them often weaken rather than advance the cause for the market, and the doctrine loses much of its halo especially after the 2007–8 crash which incidentally almost totally discredits the efficient market hypothesis.

Further Justification and Defence of the Market

Let us for the time being brush aside both the fiction-like idealisations and the ideological preachings and take a neutral and balanced view of the market. In this regard, there is still much to say in its favour both pragmatically and philosophically.

Thanks to its co-ordinating power, the first virtue of the market is its efficiency, both operation-wise and information-wise. Efficiency means not only that resources will go to where value and profit lie, but also that more transactions can be conducted within a given span of time, hence reducing the cost of transaction.

Conversely, it means that more value is added or created within that span of time. Additionally, it also means that market participants are given opportunities to spot their mistakes more quickly and correct them accordingly. Thus one can say that the market is not only efficient in terms of resource allocation, but is also efficient in terms of value creation and learning.

Another pragmatic justification of the market is the competition it fosters. On the one hand, competition imposes discipline on the market participants, eliminating the inefficient elements, thereby reducing waste of societal resources. On the other hand, competition unleashes potential for creativity and innovation. Indeed, competition and efficiency inherent in the market process can be regarded as its twin defining or signature features and by corollary, among the most important drivers behind growth.

A further corollary of market competition is that individuals are de facto held responsible for their own success or failure. This is congenial to the notion of personal accountability in our present-day regime of liberalism and individualism. While the very operation of the market presupposes non-coercive decisions and choices of the individual, the collective market outcomes reflect fully individual choices. This being the case, it is only fair and natural that market allocation of reward goes hand in hand with personal accountability. Thus it follows that true individualism must be inseparable from market individualism.

Friedman brings the argument one step further. He argues that without economic freedom, political freedom could hardly be achieved. This means that in order to safeguard our dearly treasured political institutions of liberty and democracy, we have to strive for and protect their necessary pre-condition, namely, a freely functioning market system. In a similar vein, Sen also argues that "the merit of the market does not lie only in its capacity to generate more efficient culmination outcomes, but in the processes by which those outcomes are achieved" (1999). Additionally, human hope, which represents a fundamental human condition and which helps us tide over periods of austerity, is also embedded and abundantly provided for in a free economy.

The value of the market can be further elucidated using my twin risk and value ascertainability framework. One special feature of the market is that transactions can be broken down into different sizes to fit the resource endowment and risk profile of participants. By breaking down these transactions into smaller units, value can be rendered more ascertainable and risk more containable. This state of affairs, in turn, conduces to the stepping up of the scale of transactions in the market.

"Market Forms" and a General Theory of Market Failure

But we all know that the market, in spite of its many merits, also has wide-ranging drawbacks. We have market incompleteness (e.g. goods that no private suppliers are willing to provide because of fee collection problem), market imperfections of different kinds and origins (e.g. the inability to exclude non-buyers, to prevent monopolising activities), and non-competitive markets (e.g. prices cannot reflect true social cost, informational asymmetry, principal–agent problem, time-inconsistent preferences) and so on.

All these features affect, to different extents, the efficient operation of the market and they come generally under the heading "market failure". Even the market fundamentalists admit reluctantly and occasionally these failings, although they have a stereotyped method of explaining away some of these problems (chiefly by attributing them to government intervention or government failure).

I will not be going into details regarding these highly familiar themes. It suffices just to make a few comments. First, existing theories on market failures do not fall generally into a coherent and unifying framework. They are either segmented or otherwise segregated into categories with little inter-connectedness, some related to the nature of the market, some to the nature of the goods and some to the nature of the exchange.

Second, market failure theorists tend to take the position that market failures, namely, situations where the individual pursuit of self-interest leads to outcomes that are Pareto sub-optimal, have only limited impact. They would argue or take for granted that these failures, being mostly of a local nature, have little global impact on the market system as a whole. They tend to believe that there always exist feasible solutions for correcting such failures once they are identified and their effects properly deciphered.

I think this is a grave mistake. It is true that many failures in the individual market have only local impacts. But it is possible that the cumulative effects of these failures can have, collectively and systematically, global and far-reaching consequences, among which a financial collapse can be counted as one of them. For convenience, let me label the conventional micro-structural approach to market failure as Market Failure I and the macro-dynamic approach to market failure as Market Failure II. Before I turn to the macro-dynamic analysis, let me first deal with Market Failure I from a broader framework based on the price–value analytics that has been developed.

Conventional economic theory chooses to avoid discussing value and to address the question of market efficiency from the stance of price. But a full-fledged discussion of market failure cannot avoid bringing back the parameter of value. In fact this is what has been done by some market failure theorists. I now propose to study market failure from the price–value stance instead of the conventional efficiency paradigm.

Let me start from the fundamental. I posit that a specific set of relationship between prices, values and risks in a market, i.e. how they interact and affect one another and how far prices reflect real values and risks, defines that particular "market form". This is somewhat analogous to the idea of "land form" in geology. Varying sets of price–value–risk relationships and interactions create different "market forms" with different characteristics.

The "standard market form" is, of course, one where the price–value relationship is clearly visible so much so that a buyer can readily perceive the gaps between price, expected value and realised value and act accordingly. The resulting change in overall demand compels suppliers to respond by way either of price or quality adjustment. In this standard market form, price and value operate in a self-equilibrating manner.

This "standard form" apart, there exist many other market forms where real value is less visible and therefore has a weaker link with price. I have already analysed in some detail market forms caused by rent-seeking activities which fall under the categories of soft scarcity engineering (Rent I) and hard scarcity engineering (Rent II). I have also pointed out why the labour market is a very special "market form". The labour market is comparatively inefficient because being a market with much heterogeneity in its inputs, there are multiple aspects of value on the part of both the employer and the employee that are not easy to ascertain and thereby to match. The exorbitantly high salary of CEOs of large corporations is a case in point. I have also pointed out how in the later stage of a financial cycle, the financial market undergoes a metamorphosis into a new market form, namely Finance II, where real value becomes too volatile to be visible and where liquidity rather than economic fundamental becomes the determining and driving factor of asset pricing. In these cases, mispricing is the norm rather than the exception.

Market failure as studied by the New Institutional Economics implicitly and rightly follows the rule that the more difficulty market participants experience in ascertaining value and risk, the more likely markets will fail. Factors that render value less transparent and ascertainable in the eyes of market participants include information asymmetry, the existence of a third-party agent in a transaction, unclear or incomplete property rights, high and uncertain transaction cost and so on. Also since the individual usually takes little interest in ascertaining societal value (for example the environment or non-renewable resources) or is perhaps even ignorant of them, his perceptions and decisions in this regard are governed largely by his personal interests. This explains why some markets fail to take into account social and public cost. As a matter of fact, it is abundantly clear that the market fails to account for all actual costs in the prices we pay at the checkout counter. In other words, in each of the above cases, the failure of a particular "market form" reflects the nature and degree of its value and risk ascertainability. But in spite of the fact that the market failure theorist may sometimes get it correct in his insight and diagnosis, he remains largely an optimist in the belief that these failures are not contagious. He tends to believe that as long as these failures are limited in their scope, the damages are containable. And if we can focus on identifying the sources that contribute to the non-ascertainability of the relevant values and risks, we stand a good chance of finding an effective solution.

But the disturbing part of market failure, which I call Market Failure II, is more of a systemic and global nature caused by the dynamics of growth, resulting in the emergence of subversive corporate forms, or categorically put, "corporate failure". I have in the last chapter gone into some detail how market efficiency and growth empower the rich and their agents, i.e. corporations, by endowing them with vast rent-extracting capability. I have shown how the financial sector in its developmental momentum gathers both in strength and destructive power. I have also shown how all these negative factors jointly lead to rising distributive disparity in income and wealth. The paradox, therefore, is that while the market does create and deliver value efficiently in the short-term, the mode of distribution that accompanies the market institution (which is justified by the latter) produces unexpectedly negative impacts on the less skilful workforce and the less resourceful group of society. Worse still, the trend is deteriorating. Seen in this perspective, we can say that most market failure theorists see merely the reduction of market efficiency caused by market incompleteness or imperfection. They do not seem to be aware of the seriousness of the failings of the market in its distributive arrangement. The Marxist or neo-Marxist is more concerned about the global nature of market failure, but his analysis is usually based on sweeping assumptions with an ideological undertone.

As a matter of fact, the market, even when seen to be operating efficiently at the micro-level, does not have the capability to maintain distributive neutrality. It does not prevent the growth of rent-extracting activities. Instead, it empowers the rich and impoverishes the poor. It does not smooth out economic cycles and bring about long-lasting stability to the economy. Quite the contrary, the financial market destabilises the economy and brings along devastating wealth-destroying effects, with the less resourceful suffering the most. All these are pointing to the "wholesale" failure of Market Failure II, which dwarfs all other local market failures.

In a sense, Market Failure II can be likened to the state of affairs posited by Darwinian competition. Whereas in the Smithian invisible hand narrative where competition transforms private vice into public good, Darwinian competition may turn out to be a Red Queen Race leading to no real improvement of welfare for everyone at the end of the day. This is because the relative advantage gained by an individual will eventually be caught up and cancelled out by that of others. When the Red Queen race finally stabilises, no one is really better off. In the worst possible case, the entire species may be saddled with an absolute handicap when the dust settles (as in the paradigmatic case of outsized antlers of bull elk).[5] Market Failure II, being of a systemic and dynamic nature, may come near to such a negative state of affairs, with its cumulative effects building up along with economic growth, leading to the eventual slowing down of the growth engine itself, partly by virtue of the huge maldistribution generated.

It should also be quite clear from my analysis that Market Failure II lies at the lower end of the causal chain of growth, i.e. it is the manifest outcome of growth and the subversive effects of corporate activities. In this regard, conventional studies of market failure can be said to be putting the cart before the horse. To put things in the right perspective, it is the corporations endowed with growth-inducing "institutional genes" in both the real and the financial sectors giving rise to new market forms with increasing value and risk invisibility that ultimately lead to many different forms of Market Failure I and eventually to the "wholesale" Market Failure II. In a sense, J. K. Galbraith's emphasis on the active role played by the powerful corporation is an insightful point of departure. But the paradox is that without these inherent growth-propelling "institutional genes", these corporations would not have played such a big role in fostering growth. In short, we may call this the "paradox of growth", namely, some types of Market Failure I and Market Failure II is the necessary price to be paid by or even the very condition for rapid growth. One watershed in the transition, in my bold surmise, is probably the emergence of the multi-level shareholding company which provides financiers the golden hunting ground to reap extensive rent both for the former and themselves through financial engineering. Another watershed is probably the switch in the corporate form of major investment banks from partnerships into public companies in pursuit of scale expansion, which unwittingly encourages extensive and highly leveraged risk-taking.

Thus the optimism of the conventional market failure theorist is unjustified.[6] Such optimism arises perhaps from a cognitive asymmetry, i.e. their failure to perceive in a balanced manner the halo-crowned supremacy of the market on the one hand and the apparently innocuous and redeemable local and segmented failures of individual markets (Market Failure I) on the other. Hopefully, with a new understanding of the seriousness of Market Failure II and its origin, we can have a more balanced view of the nature of the market. Formidable though the market may look in its operative efficiency, we should realise that since it also lies at the receiving point of the causal chain, it stands ample chances of being subverted by the growing power of the corporation in the longer run. Admittedly this is an economic illusion of a grand order.

A Brief Note on the Logic of Market Rationality

This is not the place to discuss the broad issue of rationality. However, a discussion of market power and market failure would be more comprehensive if we reflect on the issues from the perspective of rationality. The pertinent question is how far does the market process with economic actors acting out of enlightened self-interest yield rational outcomes? Alternatively put, will the economic man together with a free market yield the most desirable economic outcome?

The answer is probably no. The assumption that the economic actor is acting out of enlightened self-interest is made at the level of intention and potential. It means merely that the economic actor will use the best of his resources to pursue his self-interest. It has not considered the complexities at the level of execution, nor the unintended results at the level of outcome. The main problem lies at the level of execution, where the actor confronts two limitations. The first is the constraint imposed by the situation faced by the actor, which by nature is option-limiting. The second is the constraint imposed by the cognitive capability of the actor. The structural constraints imposed by a situation on the actor include such features as information inadequacy, informational asymmetry, information cost, principal–agent relationship, value invisibility, risk invisibility, non-ascertainability of transaction cost and so on. Each of these constraints may lead to serious discrepancies between the expected outcome and the actual outcome.

Expectedly, the economic actor has limited time and energy to meet the challenge of a situation, considering in particular the fact that non-response to a situation is itself a convenient response. Given the limited resources an actor commands, as well as the set of constraints imposed by the situation, including the limited range of options that the situation can offer, it is quite unlikely that the actor, in spite of his good intention, can make the shrewdest decision each and every time. Metaphorically put, the situation, with its option-limiting property, acts like a "tyrant" on him during the process of execution.

The cognitive traits of the actor acting as constraints on his judgment and decision have been extensively researched. They include induction bias, over-generalisation, misplaced concreteness, leap of logic, under-sampling, the fallacy of composition, just to mention a few (e.g. Kahneman, 2011). Of crucial significance is the fact that most actors, while quite sure about where their interest lies at any point in time, may not have a true grasp of their interest beyond the short or medium term. Given these two sets of mutually reinforcing constraints, little wonder the final outcome can turn out to be substantially different from the initial expectation of the actor.

The story does not end here. An actor may not be facing the same situation in the next round of events even if the subsequent situation may look similar and familiar. The outcome of collective actions that materialises from an earlier round, whether rational or sub-rational, shapes and defines a new round of situation, to which the actor naturally finds it necessary to respond. Since his responses are made under the above sets of constraints, some of them may turn out to be less-than-rational. Some of these less-than-rational effects may then pass on to another round of situation.[7] This means that even if an actor may have made the best out of a situation, some of the less-than-rational elements may stay on and be transmitted to define a new round of situation. Over time and collectively, these less-than-rational effects may start to accumulate, leaving less and less room for rational choice in further rounds in spite of the fact that for each and every situation taken individually and separately, the actor may still be choosing rationally.

This situation is paradigmatic in the case of bubble formation in a financial cycle. As Risk II advances and gathers momentum, the market is set for an irreversible path with narrowing scope for choice. With the deadweight of history becoming the dominant factor, investors simply have to "continue dancing until the music stops". The "tyranny" of the situation thus kicks off an option-closing process in a path-dependent manner. As a result, the freedom to choose rationally on the part of the actor and the free-functioning appearance on the part of the market becomes mere illusion. The actor may still be rational both in intention and in the sense of making the best out of any particular situation, but the market definitely is no longer so. The eventual drying up of liquidity in a financial market precipitating a financial crisis is thus probably the outcome not so much of a sudden shortage of capital but of the unsustainable and unrealistically high asset price built up over time.

In other words, even ignoring the unintended consequences of aggregation, given the above twin set of constraints, the economic man acting out of enlightened self-interest and acting in a free market, is not guaranteed to achieve rationality of outcome, especially under extreme market conditions, as in the case of a financial market moving on the way to collapse. The veil of ignorance is simply too engrossing and enveloping for the "rational" acts of the individual to pierce through.

3.2 Government–market Complementarity as Non-solution for Inequality

Naive Eclecticism

The naivety of taking solely the market or the government as a solution to economic problem is long over. Just as the idea of the command economy through central planning is finally discredited by the Soviet experience, the idea of the completely autonomous and spontaneous market is, or should be, once and for all discredited by the 2007–8 financial crisis (or at least in the financial sector). The rise of emerging nations in the past several decades embracing a heavy dose of government action, speaks clearly for the need of government–market complementarity. Except perhaps for the ultra-conservative, it is generally recognised that market failures require government remedy (whether or not we can find the right solution is another issue). Similarly, government failures can, to some extent, be alleviated by bringing in market solutions (witness the contribution of privatisation). The question that remains to be answered, it seems, is how much of each and which part of each.

While the need for government–market complementarity to solve the distribution problem is no longer disputed, the optimal dose of solution required remains highly controversial. Generally speaking, we can distinguish three competing models or approaches.

a The mixed economy with the market playing a leading role. The basic idea is to employ the market to drive growth, with the government focusing chiefly on the re-distributive job.

b State capitalism with both the government and state-owned or state-run enterprises playing a leading role. While the market is to be extensively and expediently employed, planning, policy formulation and resource allocation by the government are to play a significant role in shaping the direction of the economy.

c The Social Democratic approach or its near relative, Neo-capitalism, which blends key elements of free capital with some planning. The system can be viewed as an extreme form of mixed economy with a relatively heavy dose of government intervention. Some scholars see the kind of collaboration between government and business, such as practised in Germany and South Korea, as some kind of way out.

Why State Capitalism Cannot Sustain its Success

The recent success of some emerging nations, notably China, raises hope that the government has a big role to play both in growth and distribution. On the part of growth, I have already gone into some depth on what role the government can play, especially in the earlier stage of institutional change and scale expansion. In the later phase when productivity growth begins to take the lead, spontaneous actions of the mass in the realm of learning, innovation and creativity gradually take centre stage. Even where government policy measures are relevant, the driving force at this stage comes more from the individual. In other words, the importance of government is not a constant nor should it be. It varies with particular stages of growth and development. Should the state sector happen to constitute a significant portion of the economy after it enters the stage of maturity, the widespread disincentives inherent in this sector and its relative incompetence in innovation would likely drag down the growth of the economy.

Additionally, the insights that the public choice school has developed about bureaucracy and government failures are especially applicable to state capitalism, in particular how bureaucratic interests and behaviours lead to market inefficiency and failure. Not only that. The state sector which commands a disproportionately large bargaining and rent-extracting power would lead increasingly to conspicuous sectoral pay differentials. It is true that the state sector is relatively well-placed to create jobs but the question is one of long-term sustainability. And should the growth of the economy be on the decline due to a slowdown in overall productivity growth, polarisation among the workforce will intensify. Workers outside the state sector will be the ones that bear the brunt of the impact. Furthermore, diminished growth means slower growth of revenue, thus reducing the state's capability to perform its re-distributive function.

Worse still, the huge economic power conferred on the state sector also means that the latter has substantial political muscle to block the re-distributive plans of the government in favour of the less privileged. Over time, the tensions developed may result in a "dual economy" with negative political and social ramifications. Interestingly, recent developments have taken a new turn after the 2007–8 financial crisis. Giant state-owned enterprises, which have been enjoying ascendency and popularity in the stock market over the past two decades, have seemingly fallen out of fashion world-wide, although vicissitudes in their fate are not uncommon. This can be partly attributed to their less competitive corporate culture compared with that of their counterparts in the freer markets.

The Inefficacy of the Social Democratic Approach

Occupying the middle ground in the reform spectrum between the pole of the mixed economy and that of state capitalism are proposals coming under the banner of social democracy or neo-capitalism etc., which aim to find a third way of addressing the twin problems of market and government failure. Recall that one defining characteristic of the mixed economy is that government would abstain from meddling with the market process as far as possible. While the government is to take full responsibility of looking after the truly under-privileged at the end-point of the market process as well as to provide a reasonable level of public goods to enhance equality of opportunities in society, for example investments in education and physical infrastructure at the starting point of the market process, it is advised not to intervene directly with market operations and the pricing mechanism. On the other hand, state capitalism takes on a highly instrumental view of the market. While the market is to be exploited for its efficiency, what types of economic activities are to be left to the market and what kind of markets should be created remain the arch decisions of the central planning authority.

In contrast to the above "polarised" positions, social democracy, while advocating to retain the presence of the market as far as possible, is equally keen to address its failures and its runaway propensities. But, it is sceptical of a huge government role as in the case of state capitalism. In this regard, the basic strategy recommended would be to maintain checks and balances within the economy among its key stakeholders, i.e. corporations, trade unions, the government as well as other influential social groups prevalent in a civil society. Alternatively put, social democracy aims to use both capitalism and the market to ensure that capitalism can satisfy a diversity of human ends beyond what the market can achieve, through stronger representation of the interests of the relatively powerless groups of society as well as of the workforce through more powerful trade unions.

In a sense, the approach advocated by social democracy is in line with the kind of "corporatism" as traditionally practised in Western Continental Europe, a kind of economic system that allows big business, big labour and big government to intervene with market operations or even market outcomes (Phelps, 2013). Compared with the more market-driven system like the US, the distinct advantage is that the checks and balances of economic power within the system can help moderate the level of unemployment and inequality. But then it lacks the kind of dynamism and innovative power of the former.

Briefly summarised, while the mixed economy can be said to be characterised by "Big Market cum Small Government" and state capitalism by "Big Government cum Small Market", social democracy is characterised by "Big Government, Big Labour cum Big Market". Sadly, with the gradual impoverishment of labour world-wide as a result of globalisation, technological progress as well as the ascendency of orthodox neo-liberalism in recent decades, social democracy has lost much of its support. Some scholars, however, still see the doctrine as a useful antidote to unfettered capitalism. Colin Crouch, for example, proposes to transcend the doctrine from a defensive to a more assertive level by rebuilding the strength of trade unions and other groups in a civil society (2013). While the goal is laudable, it is doubtful whether with the decline of labour, such programmes can stand up to the power of capital and its corporate agents backed up by the formidable ideology of neo-liberalism. As a matter of fact, even countries in North Western Europe with an impressive egalitarian record are experiencing higher levels of inequality, although they still look good on a relative basis.

The Mixed Economy and the Enfeeblement of the Government

There is no need to dwell at length on this subject. The analysis I have made in the preceding sections on the market economy is fully applicable to the market side of the mixed economy. The additional question that I would like to focus upon is how in a mixed economy, the government will become crippled to the extent that it is gradually losing its capability to carry out fully its re-distributive function, a function which is so essential to maintaining some kind of equity and balance in a civil society.

The first point is, as the public choice school has argued in depth, given the opportunistic behaviours of politicians and bureaucrats in their implementation of policies, however well-intentioned and well-designed these policies may be, it is not necessarily the case that their outcomes can correct or make up for the inadequacies or failures of the market. Broadly speaking, this is the principal–agent problem in one of its different manifestations. Supervisory authorities can turn out to be the prisoners of the entities that they control and that they are supposed to supervise. Briefly put, it is likely that they are "captured" by private interest. In addition, partisan ideologies and politics can easily bias economic policy, putting political ends and considerations above economic well-being and development.

The main problem with the operation of the mixed economy, however, lies not merely in the gullibility of bureaucrats or the ideological bent of the politicians, but also in the growth dynamics I have analysed. After all, there are still many checks and balances in a liberal or constitutional democracy, for example an independent judiciary or its active media. An electorate that can legitimately dispose of a government, competing political parties vying for power, a well-established legal system and so on, should in principle be powerful enough to exercise considerable constraint on the behaviours of politicians and bureaucrats. The problem, as has already been analysed, lies rather in the gradual tilting of the balance of economic power along with the growth of the economy, as an increasingly huge proportion of societal resources go into the hands of the rich, the capital owners and the big firms. Bureaucrats, being just human, can hardly resist the temptation and their being captured by growing private interests is probably a matter of time. From then on, the mixed economy moves on to become a "mixed failure economy" where market failures join force with government failures, with each side reinforcing the other in a negative feedback loop. Increasing distributive disparity is the inevitable outcome of this new partnership even without the negative impact of the financial cycle, ushering in a new era of the "politics of anger" that we now witness across the developed countries.

Increasing distributive inequality in a "mixed-failure economy" means that aggregate demand is not likely to be sufficient to meet aggregate supply and thereby to sustain the normal working of the economy, let alone fostering a healthy rate of growth. Following the Keynesian logic, the economy would then be trapped in a low-level equilibrium unless the government steps in. Any democratic government facing this situation has little choice but to adopt an expansionary policy either by way of boosting spending or by way of pursuing easy monetary policy or by a combination of both. In fact, even without the pressure of inadequate aggregate demand and its threat in generating a recession, the modern liberal democracy is naturally prone to please its voters who always want more. When bureaucrats and politicians join hands with capital owners in the extractive game, the "wisest" thing to do would be for the government to spend more and more public money to pacify the voters. Thus, to keep spending far beyond its means is an expedient that a government intending to remain in power cannot resist, until it discovers that it cannot borrow easily and cheaply any more.

Debt surge and pile-up cannot go on forever. Economists differ in their estimates regarding the debt an economy can put up with without being trapped in a state of stagnation. Whichever is the critical debt/GDP ratio, or whether or not there exists a definitive ratio, or whether it takes a catalyst to trigger off a crisis once the ratio is passed, debt build-up does distort the normal working of an economy. Public debt may crowd out private borrowing and investment. To keep down the servicing cost, any government that has the power to manipulate interest rates will try to maintain as low an interest regime as possible. But keeping a low interest regime has a long-term cost. It misprices capital and distorts its allocation. It drives up asset prices and induces the formation of bubble in the financial markets. Even after a bubble has burst, a continuing low interest rate policy that is needed to prevent an economy from falling into a recession still gives the capital owners an edge. In short, capital keeps enjoying more advantage than labour under a long-stretched low interest or loose monetary policy regime coupled with and sustained by high levels of debt. This, needless to say, aggravates indefinitely distributive disparity between capital and labour.

This is not the place to give a critical account of current events and topical affairs. But as the US experience in the post-2007–8 crisis reveals, not even a sustained low interest regime can kick an economy off a recession easily. The de-leveraging process is so deep and extensive that the Federal Reserve eventually resorts to using a direct method, namely, quantitative easing (QE) to engineer a recovery. How successful this method eventually is remains to be seen, partly because the process of exit has not been completed. With the effectiveness of monetary policy partly crippled, the logical alternative or supplement is to employ more extensively the Keynesian dose, namely, a discretionary fiscal policy. But this has the likelihood of pushing the government further into debt. Some Keynesians like Paul Krugman argue that debts do not really matter (2013). In their opinion, the right thing the government must do and do quickly is to push up aggregate demand and the rest will take care of itself.

Granted that the Keynesians are correct in principle that in a state of recession, the government should spend quickly and generously to get its economy out of it, especially when monetary policy turns out to be less-than-effective, there are still questions to consider. This is because the value and effectiveness of the fiscal policy multiplier depend on the state of the economy and the character of other economic policies that are presently in force. Among others, some issues to consider include the following:

a   Whether government spending works equally effectively in a state of high indebtedness; note that an economy that is relatively debt-free has a greater flexibility to boost spending in a downturn and most of today's Western nations have seemingly lost that flexibility;

b   What proportion of policy-induced increase in household disposable income is likely to be saved;

c   What level of excess supply an economy is experiencing;

d   Whether it is likely that a growing level of debt would trigger a sudden fiscal crisis, for example when investors lose confidence in government's ability to manage its debt;

e   Whether government spending can yield a reasonable level of productive value. This is because while fiscal stimulus has a clear short-term effect, it is doubtful if it has a long-term positive effect on GDP growth unless the key supply-side factors that boost productivity can be fundamentally improved;

f   Whether the level of revenue to be generated by the recovery will be more than adequate to pay back for the debt thus incurred within a particular time-frame.[8]

As a matter of fact, one pending problem faced by many governments in the industrial world is that their long-term revenue generating ability is on the decline. What with ageing population, a possible down-trend in technological innovation, chronic unemployment eroding human capital formation, especially among the young, a disproportionately low level of investment in physical infrastructure – many of these "supply-side" factors are of a structural nature and are not easy to remedy even with bigger government spending, let alone an expansionary monetary policy.

The European nations are in a particularly difficult situation. Unlike their US counterpart, the room for them to print money is relatively limited. As can be expected, the borrowing cost demanded by the global capital market reflects more or less its perception of the ability of a nation to service its debt or of the risk of default. Between the devil and the deep blue sea, some of the hard-hit nations understandably resort to austerity measures to contain their levels of debt. But apart from the threat of recession, one serious negative consequence of austerity measures is that they tend to hurt the less resourceful and the less skilled disproportionately. Relentless pursuit of these measures pushes inevitably these economies to ever higher levels of inequality, which, in the longer run, may further slow down growth.

As has already been pointed out, even in the case of say, the US, where debt is denominated in local currency, debt building, which can last for a very long-stretched period, cannot go on forever. Mounting debt strengthens the bargaining power of creditors until debtor nations resort to using extra-ordinary measures including inflation, devaluation or even default. But these measures, especially the last one, are becoming less palatable in today's global economy and are at best temporary solutions.

To sum up, present-day governments are, for various reasons, becoming more enfeebled. Many of them cannot even solve the problem of spurring growth, let alone the problem of inequality which works in an interlocking circle with declining growth. Also, as a result of their general impotence in managing economic affairs, politicians are easily losing their credibility as well as their moral high ground. To get elected or to stay on the job, they often have to bow to the short-term demands of their electorate, meaning more welfare dole-out and more government spending. And the vicious circle goes on. The picture is more dismal if one takes into account the fact that the supply-side factors haunting these nations are structural in nature.

Specially worthy of mention is the world's demographic trend with its disturbing consequences. An ageing economy as we know has significant impact on both equality and growth. According to UN statistics, the share of world population by those above 65 will grow from 8% today to 13% by 2035, or more than 1.1 billion people. The "old-age dependency ratio" will grow from 15 people for every 100 adult now to 26 by 2035.

Assuming present policies remain pretty much the same, this means not only slower growth, but also higher interest rates and lower asset prices as the old will have to draw down their wealth to keep a living and there will be less savings. Moreover, among the ageing group, the less skilled workers that depend on manual work for their income will drop out fast with ageing while those high skilled will extend their working life. This further aggravates income and wealth disparity.

To address the above problems and to solve at once the twin problems of growth and inequality, a new thinking is needed.

Notes

1 Smith is actually quite cool-headed and sophisticated. He sees quite clearly that the normal operations of the economy might create a group of people who would be able to hi-jack it. Thus he sees a strong role for government from punishing dishonest acts to regulating finance and to providing education and public order.

2 One interesting case is that when a new technology comes along with a great deal of uncertainty, investors, in order not to miss the boat, tend to spread their bets on the newcomers into the game. The net effect would be that, in aggregate, the valuation of the sector will become ridiculously high and eventually turn the market into a bubble.

3 Of interest is the argument that if the EMH were true, there would be no need to invest in research because the market would, almost by magic, have beaten us all.

4 Some scholars, however, are sceptical of his view, Walter Block, for example, argues that Hayek's "The Road to Serfdom" is quite lukewarm in its support of a free market system (1996).

5 This prompts Robert Frank (2011) to predict that within the next century, Charles Darwin will take over Adam Smith as the intellectual founder of economics.

6 In his work *The Price of Inequality*, Joseph Stiglitz argues that in recent decades, market forces interplaying with political machinations in the US, lead to deteriorating distributive disparity. Bringing the argument further, he takes the strong position that markets by themselves, even when they are stable, lead to high levels of inequality outcomes. By implication, he is also advancing a general theory of market failure, namely, markets have an inherent tendency to fail and it is therefore up to the government to correct this state of affairs. My view is that while he is largely correct in his diagnosis, he has taken too strong a position, especially in that he puts too much trust in the role of government in making up for such deficiencies. My analysis differs from his in two important ways. First, in my scheme of explanation, not all "market forms" are equally prone to failure. In general, market forms that have a lower degree of value and risk ascertainability are more prone to failure. Second, given the widening power asymmetry between capital and market driven by growth, government has a diminishing capability to arrest the degeneration, apart from the fact that more government may generate new problems of governance.

7 George Soros chooses to call this feature "reflexibility", which can operate either in a negative or positive feedback loop.

8 Some economists calculate the cost-benefit by counting the loss of output and human capital as a result of low-level employment of the factor inputs of the economy.

4 The NPV Model and Economy II

4.1 The Paradox and Predicaments of the Capitalist System

What I have done in Part I of this book amounts to giving an informal "proof" that the capitalist system that is practised today in most countries (I will term it "Economy I" hereafter) is not tenable in two ways. They are:

a   The Impossibility Thesis: Modern capitalism (Economy I) cannot deliver the twin goals of growth and equality (or less inequality to be more exact) simultaneously.
b   The Non-sustainability Thesis: Even if Economy I can achieve growth and spread prosperity, it can do so for only a limited period. The dynamics of Economy I would result over time in deteriorating distributive disparity which drags down overall growth.

If Economy I is doomed in delivering satisfactorily these twin goals, do we have to abandon it altogether? Can its shortcomings be repaired? Or is this scenario the best that humanity can ever get? Or, if we were to abandon it, what should we put in its stead?

The first answer to these questions is that by the Impossibility Thesis, Economy I, even if its obvious drawbacks can be repaired, still cannot deliver the aspired twin goals. Yes, many shortcomings and overshoots of the system can be mended to yield more positive results. But as I have shown, many problems of Economy I are brought about by economic illusions arising from economic growth, the grandest and most pervasive of which is that we tend to take price to faithfully reflect value, whereas in actual fact, value has in many markets become seriously distorted. Even if we work hard to correct this cognitive bias in each and every sector, the huge and widening asymmetry of economic power between capital and labour, as caused by the sustained operation of modern "corporate forms" in both the real and the financial sector, is hardly repairable under the existing capitalist regime. This means that in the long run, substantial inequality will stay on, even if it does not worsen over time.

If so, do we have to subscribe to the Marxist or neo-Marxist view that we have to do away with capitalism altogether and replace it with something else? The answer to this long-asked and almost boring question is, of course, a resounding no. Half a century of experiment under the directive of central planning or command in different places and among different races has shown clearly that such an alternative cannot deliver robust medium-term growth, let alone true equality.

The reason is that the present capitalist system, despite its inability in managing the problem of inequality, is probably by far the best we have in fostering economic growth and development. The "capitalist formula" of Economy I consists in three essential components.

a   The market: By virtue of its high visibility of risk and value, the market provides the most efficient platform for production and exchange.
b   The firm: The establishment of the modern joint-stock company with limited liability is well equipped both to take risk and to enlist capital resources. It is the "very" engine of growth by virtue of its "institutional genes".
c   The government: By virtue of its role in supporting both (a) and (b), namely the protection of property rights via the rule of law and proper functioning of the market.

In some cases, the strategic plans and actions of government also play a positive role in driving growth.

Obviously we cannot do away with any of the above three components if we want the overall growth engine to function effectively. Hence we need to keep Economy I. But on the other hand, we have shown how the growth dynamics of Economy I cannot stop maldistribution from taking place and worsening over time. The paradox, therefore, is that there appears to be a trade-off between prosperity and inequality. Worse still, the long-term picture is more dismal than that of a simple trade-off, for inequality will in turn slow down growth and enfeeble government over time, as I have taken pains to show in Part One of this book.

4.2 NPV Model and Economy II

But it need not be that dismal. This is because we can build a second economy (hereafter to be termed "Economy II") side by side with Economy I.[1] The basic idea is to split the overall capitalist economy into two sectors, the conventional one, i.e. Economy I and a new insulated sector, Economy II. Economy II is characterised by the operation of the most simple market form (i.e. the truly self-equilibrating market with prices converging towards value and vice versa) and the most primitive corporate form (companies formed and operated by natural persons only). The two sectors are to be partitioned by a "firewall" to prevent the penetration of the negative elements and effects of Economy I into Economy II. However, the benefits to be derived from Economy II, while itself being a self-contained sector, can be allowed to flow into Economy I. That is, the traffic between Economy I and II is "semi-one-way".

The question now is by what means and resources are we going to invent or construct Economy II and by what kind of method we are to separate the two sectors? The two basic ideas I am going to employ are the natural person (as opposed to the legal person or more precisely the juridical person)[2] and the voucher (as opposed to direct money subsidy). Juridical persons are treated by law as if they were real persons. Economy II is to be operated solely and strictly by the most primitive "corporate form" to be formed and operated solely by and among natural persons (in other words, all legal or juridical persons are barred). The buying power in Economy II at the initial stage is provided by the government in the form of vouchers that it issues. To ensure a level playing field, a natural person is allowed to operate only one business or company in Economy II. He is not allowed to hold any share of the business of any other natural persons. He is, however, permitted to hold shares of all kinds of companies in Economy I. Also he can join force with a small, limited number of natural persons to form and operate a "natural person partnership company". But once he does so, he can no longer own or operate a natural person company. Nor is he allowed to hold shares of more than one natural person partnership company. He may sell his shares upon the agreement of his other natural person partners but he is not allowed to start a new natural person company as long as he holds shares in a natural person partnership company.

The reason why Economy II bars the entry of legal or juridical persons (regardless of how shareholdings are structured) is that there is a large asymmetry between the power possessed by other "corporate forms", for example the legal person company including the private limited liability company, public company (corporation) and that of the natural person company. Interwoven with and underlying the ideas of the legal person company are the ideas of stock and limited liability. The stock of a company or corporation constitutes the equity stake of its owners. Under such a design the ownership of the company or corporation is legally divisible into small units, i.e. shares, and these shares can be separately owned and freely transferred. As early as the Roman Republic, the state leased out some of its services to private companies which are similar to modern corporations or joint-stock companies.

The limited liability company was invented in sixteenth-century Europe, and was known in its early days as the joint-stock company. The earliest recognised joint-stock company in modern times was the English East India Company. But it was not until the mid-nineteenth century, beginning with Sweden in 1844 and followed by Britain in 1856 that the countries of Western Europe and North America made limited liability generally available. With the wider adoption of this institutional design since the late nineteenth century and early twentieth century, capital accumulation and technological progress accelerated at an unprecedented pace, signifying the advent of the era of "corporate capitalism".

The status of legal person combining features of joint ownership and limited liability confer on this new "corporate form", be it a limited liability company or a corporation, an incredible ability to expand. Having the status of legal person means that the modern firm acquires a "corporate personhood", meaning business can now survive the removal or death of its founder. Limited liability sets a ceiling to the potential loss of a company. Importantly, it implies the imposition of an asymmetry between risk and return. The "taming" of risk via limiting loss only to subscribed or invested capital means capital owners now have far more to gain than to lose in their business ventures. Joint ownership in the form of divisible shareholdings, on the other hand, can attract investors small and big alike, not only because it is easy to make an investment but it is also easy to exit, hence reducing the risk of being tied up with a particular investment. New issues of shares are also permitted to raise capital to meet the needs of the company. As a result, much of the idle capital in the society is activated and channelled into productive use, spurring growth to an unprecedented high level.

Since there is no legal limit on size and since highly divisible ownership under the protection of limited liability is permitted, the modern firm is easily scalable, enabling it to reap all the advantages that a big scale of operation promises. These include risk diversification, access to credit, economies of management, production and marketing, resources to plan ahead and to invest into the future, as well as the ability to mobilise resources for research and development etc. It is, of course, true that expanding the scale of operation can also bring about a host of management problems, for example, bureaucratic rigidity in decision-making and execution or loss of personal touch with customers. But on balance, the advantages far outweigh the drawbacks.

This is only half of the story. The creation of the bank, whose "corporate form" is characterised by leverage and credit creation, signifies the entry of another growth engine, which in due course gives rise to modern finance. Modern finance brings along a new synergy with the modern firm by giving the latter access to a variety of means for financing and hedging. A host of "financial engineering" techniques, such as IPO, corporate bond issues, mergers and acquisitions, leveraged buyouts etc., all enable the firm to expand in size and to create "value" for both capital owners and financial practitioners, often without even the need to raise the level or change the pattern of real production activities.

Worthy of special mention is the modern holding company, another important corporate form with profound ramifications. With the advent of the holding company, multi-layered and cross holdings of shares of different companies are possible. Such a structure nurtures and fits perfectly the techniques of modern finance. With the help of the latter, a holding company can easily build itself up into a business empire via mergers and acquisitions, with funding supplied from the financial sector. Metaphorically, this represents a perfect "marriage" between the real sector and the financial sector. The price to be paid by the emergence of such highly opaque and complex corporate structure characterising the holding company is, of course, that value visibility can become much compromised.

Notwithstanding its contribution to the development of the real economy, the financial sector also spurs a twin process of resource distraction and extraction from the real sector, which should not be lightly dismissed. As previously pointed out, the "financialisation" of the real sector results in short-termism. Capital owners and their financial "accomplices" increasingly demand handsome short-term yield often at the expense of longer-term investment and the long-term well-being of the firm. The CEOs and their top management, with executive compensations and bonuses tied to company performance, are naturally keen to comply with such an objective. To this end, they engage more intensely in manipulative and rent-seeking activities and adopt management models that unwittingly impair the well-being of the low skilled workforce. They work hand in hand with financial experts and engage relentlessly in merger and acquisition activities which more often than not, bring about short-term benefit to deal-makers, the top management and financial professionals at the expense of the long-term benefit of the firm and its employees.

The upshot of the above is that just as the advantages inherent in the big limited liability joint-stock companies and their formidable descendant, the holding companies enable them to behave as "predators" to the smaller companies, financial companies and investment banks joining force with the former also act as some kind of "predators" to other firms in the real sector, in particular the medium-sized ones or those without much financial expertise. Interestingly and in this regard, the modern corporation as a person is sometimes perceived to be inhuman and vicious, displaying such traits as consistent irresponsibility, unrepentfulness and reckless disregard for the well-being of others. There is, of course, some exaggeration in this sweeping generalisation because there always exist symbiotic relationships between the big and the small firms and between the real and the financial sector. But the fact remains that firms operating under such "modern" corporate form, interacting synergistically with the leverage-exploiting "entities" in the financial sector, while fostering growth and prosperity at the first stage of development, brings about major disruptions in the ecology of present-day capitalism in the course of time.

During the recent decades, "alternative corporate forms" emerge to sidestep the need for regulatory compliance and the high cost involved as well as to take advantage of tax loopholes. Examples of such "alternative corporate forms" include different forms of private partnerships (for example Master Limited Partnership [MLP]), Limited Liability Partnerships (LLPS), Publicly Traded Partnerships (PTPS) and Real Estate Investment Trusts (REITS), private-equity companies and family conglomerates. Some of these are "pass-through" structures. MLPS, for example, do not pay corporate taxes so long as profits are passed on to investors each year. Since the 2007–8 financial crises, these new structures become more popular with growing regulatory burden on firms. For example, Business-Development Companies (BDCS) provide credit to businesses abandoned by the banks. The advantage of minimising tax payments apart, these "pass-through" structures also enhance the flow of money and capital and give higher return to investors.

Small and medium-sized firms defined as those whose employment falls below a certain level, are generally recognised as important contributors to an economy. It is quite an irony that these companies, while registering the highest average mortality rate, also contribute importantly to employment in an economy. All in all, while these small "fishes" (some of which are sole proprietors) are making solid contributions to the economy, it is the bigger "sharks" that extract most of the benefits. The story of how this happens need not be repeated.

The idea of Economy II, then, is to erect an insulated space where only the "corporate form" of natural person company to be operated by a natural person (or that of small and limited partnership among a few individuals) is allowed. This ensures that Economy II is a far more level playing field. The important point is that this playing field is not likely to be subverted by any of its players not only because it operates chiefly via the simple, naturally self-equilibrating market form by virtue of the nature of the goods and services it provides (which require relatively little capital investment), but also because there is a limit to which an average natural person company can grow or survive long enough to dominate a market in Economy II. To further limit the size of a natural person company, we may consider setting up additional rules to restrict its realm of activities in case of need.

An issue that deserves attention is whether or not the liability of a natural person company should also be limited and to what extent. Like its counterpart in Economy I, the natural person company, if it were to be given the status of a limited liability company, can make the investor cum operator more risk prone and venturesome. If we want him to be more responsible and accountable, we can consider introducing some kind of "extended liability" by establishing some kind of formula, for example the amount of liability is limited not merely to the value of the subscribed capital of the company, but also to say, a percentage of his annual total turnover or profit.

4.3 Empowering Economy II – the Idea of Voucher

Where then does Economy II get the resources to form different markets and sub-sectors? Needless to say, the capital required has to be first financed by the government. This is done in the form of vouchers to be distributed to the target recipients. They are then used as money substitutes to buy goods and services produced within Economy II. Providers of these goods or services, upon receipt of the vouchers spent by the recipients, will claim back from the government the equivalent amount of money.

A voucher is a kind of bond which is worth a certain monetary value and which may be spent only for specific purposes or on specific goods. Examples include (but are not limited to) housing, travel, food and education vouchers. Friedman's proposal of the school voucher is a path-breaking example of how vouchers can have important market functions. The government as usual takes on the responsibility of providing public education but it can entrust the actual provision of such services to private schools that receive funding or subsidy in the form of vouchers to be issued to parents. Parents, the direct recipients of vouchers, have now the freedom to choose which schools they want to send their children to. Schools can now freely use their voucher revenue to provide services that meet the expectations of the parents who choose them. Parents can pay out of their own pocket over and above the standard value of the voucher to meet the higher fees charged by some schools that promise to provide a higher quality service. In a sense, a competitive market is created upon government spending, but one that can supposedly deliver more value to both the parents and the schools.

Economy II employs the same idea. The government is to issue vouchers to a selected group of recipients. But these vouchers can be used to buy only the goods and services and provided by natural person companies within Economy II. Customers, of course, are free to incur extra expenses on top of the voucher values for their purchases in Economy II. Natural personal companies can then plan their business ahead in line with the potential purchasing power. Markets are thus formed within Economy II on the basis of demand created by vouchers as well as of supply based on the expectations of the magnitude of the pre-announced purchasing power to be injected. Since Economy II operators can also sell their products and services to buyers in Economy I, they may also take into account the size of demand outside the circle of voucher recipients.

4.4 Operational Details of Economy II – the Natural Person Company

We have proposed that only natural person companies formed by natural persons are allowed to operate in Economy II. A natural person can own one natural person company or he can join a "natural person partnership company" with a limited number of partners (who are also natural persons), in which case he no longer has the right to own another natural person company. The latter arrangement aims to strike a balance between maintaining as far as possible a level playing field while encouraging a certain degree of division of labour and specialisation among these natural persons. On the other hand, there is no limit as to the number of employees a natural person company can hire. A natural person, apart from operating a single natural person company in Economy II, while being allowed to own shares in companies operating in Economy I, is not allowed to actively run or work in other companies in Economy I (this rule can be relaxed depending on the individual circumstances of an economy).

Should a natural person die, the assets held by his natural person company can be transferred or passed on to another natural person according to his will, but in that case, the beneficiary may have to give up the natural person company that he himself happens to own or operate. Since this process involves a transfer of interest, the government may have to design rules governing conditions and terms of transfer to satisfy both equity and incentive considerations.

In principle, a natural person company, like its legal person counterpart, should be subject to taxation. The rates of taxation, the types and amounts of concessions to be granted (including tax holidays) depend on the level of incentive a government considers appropriate. The choice is between how much short-term incentive is to be granted and the long-term revenue Economy II expects to receive.

4.5 Economy II in Operation – Vouchers

In the embryonic and formative stage, Economy II depends on the purchasing power injected by the government in the form of vouchers. By their very nature, vouchers represent promises to pay but these promises usually go with certain restrictions. To build an Economy II with specific objectives and priorities in mind, we can design two types of vouchers, "general-purpose vouchers" which apply to the entire Economy II, and can be used to purchase any kind of products or services available in Economy II and "specific-purpose vouchers" which can be used to purchase only specified products and services. While "general-purpose vouchers" are "quasi-money" and represent general purchasing power, "specific-purpose vouchers" are used additionally to encourage the supply of certain goods and services. The latter are particularly useful in nurturing those sectors which have the potential to grow robustly. The idea is somewhat similar to that of incubating infant industries. Vouchers, whether they are of the general-purpose or sector-specific kind, go beyond the mere provision of welfare. They also perform the role of market creation and thereby the role of growth driver. Unlike sheer welfare provision, they have the objective of actively spurring the less privileged class to join the economic game by granting them opportunities that match or stimulate their potential.

If the main objective consists at once in providing welfare dole-out and stimulating a broad range of suppliers, general-purpose vouchers would be more appropriate. But if the chief objective is to develop certain special markets and talents especially among the less privileged groups, special-purpose vouchers can be amply supplied. In the latter case, research studies may have to be conducted to ascertain preferences of potential voucher recipients for better matching.

Specific-purpose vouchers are, in this regard, arbitrary aggregate demand plans tailored-made to fit or shape the potential and desired supply structure of the low skilled, the less privileged and the less resourceful groups of society. The kind of products and services supplied are expectedly mainly those that meet the simple and mundane needs of everyday life. These include products and services that are relatively easy to make and provide, that do not require high cost of production and substantial physical capital outlay, that can be supplied by small groups of workers without too much technical expertise, training and organisational sophistication.

Sectors and industries that are generally suited to the application of these specific vouchers include the following: food and beverage, retailing, trading, household chores, personal coaching of different fields, health care services of a low-tech kind (e.g. some kinds of nursing), entertainment business, art business, home furnishing, design, repair and maintenance work and so on.

In other words, specific-purpose vouchers can be employed to promote a broad spectrum of labour-based and labour-intensive products and services that can be supplied without much technical sophistication and capital investment. Should the vouchers issued match well the labour endowment of an economy, we can expect Economy II to grow and mature in the following manner.

a   In the first stage, the government is to make public its voucher plans and the time frames of operation. At the same time, the government should also actively provide extensive vocational training to those who consider entering the game but lack the basic skills. Such plans and training should interest and motivate a group of people, including low skilled workers, people who are out of job, people who have already retired, and people who are actively seeking a job but cannot find one and so on. Those who are uncompetitive in Economy I or at the edge of giving up may also consider moving into this subsidised and much less competitive arena.

b   With voucher subsidies being systematically injected into Economy II, competitive markets begin to form as more people see good opportunities and are tempted to seize them. A broad spectrum of low-end products and services gradually emerge. This process is quite similar to infant industry development that leverages on initial subsidy and that gradually gains strength through cost reduction and experience acquisition. Part of the income earned by members of Economy II will be cycled back. Over time the aggregate demand within Economy II will grow via its own bootstrapping process as well as more voucher injection from government.

c   The expansion of Economy II into a mass market of different types of services, especially of the more labour-intensive kind, will eventually induce firms in Economy I to change their business focus and emphasise on industries that require new and higher technologies with more capital requirement as well as those products, the production of which requires large team collaboration or highly organised management. In time, the two economies will each specialise according to their comparative advantage, Economy I being a "technology-driven economy" and Economy II being largely a "mass service economy". While the symbiotic relationship between them on the production side is rather limited, the income and demand generated by the respective sectors will nevertheless help boost one another. The more successful natural personal companies may start investing in Economy I, while members of Economy I will increase their demand for the products and services provided by Economy II. Whichever the outcome, the big capital owners in Economy I, whatever their doings and wrong-doings, can have hardly any negative impact on Economy II.

4.6 Funding

In the initial stage of constructing of Economy II, a clear-cut time-table of when and how much funding will be injected is critical. Pre-announcing voucher plans will go a long way to encouraging those who have or who decide to garner resources to take advantage of the forthcoming business opportunities as well as those who want to acquire the basic skills to join the game to get well prepared. Should the government also inject extra funding in the form of arranging loans either directly or via banks to natural person companies, we can expect the supply-side process to be further speeded up. Whichever the case, the kick-off of Economy II does require substantial initial government spending. This may be financed by raising tax on Economy I operators or the super-rich, or by issuing government bonds, among other methods (see next section). The key point is that as Economy II makes good progress along its growth pathway, it should be able to build up some cap-ability to expand on its own resources and hopefully, generate a certain level of tax revenue to partly pay for and sustain its activities. Even if self-sustain-ability cannot be fully achieved, the deficit thus incurred will have a much higher benefit for the economy as a whole than the conventional "passive" welfare spending. That is to say, the extra government revenue raised by taxing the super-rich to be spent on Economy II should be far more effective in achieving the goal of equitable distribution for society than otherwise.

4.7 Possible Drawbacks and Criticisms

The most obvious drawback of the proposed scheme, in particular with respect to sector-specific or specific-purpose vouchers, is that it gives a lot of discretion to the voucher issuing authority. There are going to be a lot of arbitrary decisions on the supply-side. These include determining the type and the amount of vouchers, for example, how much should be allocated to gen-eral-purpose vouchers and specific-purpose vouchers, how specific-purpose vouchers are to be divided among different sectors and industries, and how these plans are to be adjusted and revised within specific time frames. One needs to bear in mind that many potential suppliers would join the game and make investment only when they are assured that these vouchers are to stay on for some specified period. This is particularly so for vouchers that are meant chiefly to stimulate the development of certain sectors or industries. Since these are highly arbitrary decisions, the skill and ability of the voucher issuing authority can make a big difference.

The above drawback is typical of any planned economic activity or of planning in general. The good news, however, is that the vouchers plans in question are to be introduced in different stages and can be subject to amendment based on feedbacks if necessary. The central voucher issuing authority can learn from its mistakes and make corrections. Provided that a sufficiently long notice is given, amendments should cause little long-term disruption. Even if the plans are far off the mark, the consequences are not going to be fatal. In the worst circumstances, they can be written off as one-off welfare dole outs. Furthermore, even an originally ill-conceived plan can have the unintended effect of creating the right kind of demand in the longer run.

Moreover, even if mistakes arising from these arbitrary decisions are not defensible, they are still more of the technical kind. This is because unlike favouritism or cronyism often practised in Economy I, officials in charge of voucher planning and issuing have little to gain personally by colluding with voucher recipients not only because the latter are small in size, but also unlike big corporations in Economy I, they are too decentralised. Like all re-distributive schemes, there will be some politics involved, but hopefully the conflicts would be of moderate extent.

Another issue is the question of the arbitrariness of voucher issue. While specific-purpose vouchers are targeted at specific social groups that the government wants to help or specific industries that the government wants to promote and are thus more arbitrary by nature, general purpose vouchers are much less so. This is because the eventual market pattern that emerges under the umbrella of general purpose vouchers is governed by the dynamic interactions between the patterns of demand on the part of the voucher recipients and the supply capability on the part of the natural person companies. By comparison, selection of projects to be sponsored by government spending under the regime of Keynesian demand management is less spontaneous, more arbitrary and less sustainable, and probably has a lower multiplier effect.

One way to minimise planning risk is to issue only general purpose vouchers in the initial stage, taking into account broadly the labour endowment and the demand structure of that particular economy. After that, the central voucher issuing authority can begin to issue sector or industry-specific vouchers based on feedback from the general purpose vouchers and other social surveys and do it on an experimental basis. This gradualist approach incurs less risk, but it will take more time to turn Economy II into a mature, fully operational system.

Another possible objection to Economy II is that the capital thus injected may crowd out both public and private investments that would have gone to Economy I, where firms, supposed to possess more skill and experience in spotting business opportunities and make better use of resources, can yield higher return. Channelling resources from sectors of higher productivity in Economy I, for example the export sector, to low-tech, low-skilled ones in Economy II may, therefore, drag down the overall performance and competitiveness of the economy as a whole. My reply is that this may well be the case in the first stage of development. But as Economy II is well on the pathway of growth, it will, on top of complementing Economy I though specialisation in areas of its comparative advantage, create more resources, especially of the human kind on its own. In the medium to long run, the bootstrapping process that ensues should enable it to stand on its own foot, resulting eventually in a win-win situation for all.

Another line of criticism is that upon the announcement of voucher plans some existing firms may face the choice of whether they should switch to the status of the natural person operator to take advantage of the forthcoming potential demand or whether they should maintain the status quo, in which case they may face loss of customers who can now opt for supply in Economy II. Since this switch is absolutely legitimate, the existing suppliers with their experiences in operation stand a good chance of winning voucher holders, rendering the newcomers who are less resourceful or less skilled disadvantaged. To strike a balance between giving existing operators the option to switch to Economy II so that supply in Economy II can be readily available in the first stage of operation and making Economy II to be as level a playing field as possible, the voucher-issuing authority may consider to limit the group of existing operators who opt for conversion of company status only to those with a business record of less than say three to five years or to those with a turnover, profit or tax paid, below a certain amount.

Another problem is that at the initial stage, it may be difficult to estimate the effect of vouchers on both the level of supply from the natural person companies and the level of employment, especially the number of workers who are willing to work in these natural person companies. Generally, these problems have to be addressed on a trial-and-error basis. In the event of say, a low rate of participation in Economy II in the first period, it may be necessary to give workers additional incentive by way of more voucher subsidy and fine-tune such a level as and when it is necessary. These technical problems, however, should by no means belittle the usefulness of the NPV scheme over a longer time frame.

The usefulness of fine-tuning subsidy to workers in Economy II goes beyond boosting the employment level in this sector. It enables government to reduce the conventional unemployment benefits or other kinds of welfare dole-out. It is therefore another case of substituting "passive welfarism" by a kind of "active welfarism" or "productive welfarism".[3] Eventually, when Economy II stands on its own feet, the extra subsidy can be withdrawn.

One prime problem to consider is, of course, funding. Critics of the scheme may argue that since the scheme requires additional funding, thereby putting even more pressure on the existing fiscal conditions of most governments, it is doubtful if it can be sustainable. On the other hand, if we are to choose the option of funding by exorbitantly raising tax, it is likely to have negative effects.

To be fair, funding can pose a real constraint to the full operation of the scheme. But the problem is far less serious than it looks. First, the scheme can be implemented by steps in line with the maximal resources that the government projects to garner and pay back realistically. Second, the scheme can be looked upon as some kind of social investment with the capability of yielding a return beyond the short term. Third, on careful scrutiny, a number of funding sources can be identified apart from issuing government bonds. These include (a) proceeds from closing existing tax loopholes; (b) more controversial is, of course, funding from higher tax rates. There are, in this regard, four possible options: (a) raising the general tax rate; (b) re-designing the existing tax structure for more progressiveness; (c) a super-tax on the rich; (d) higher penalties on sophisticated tax evaders and their money-laundering paradises. Conventional objections to these measures are that corporations and capital owners may reduce their overall level of investment or that they would lead to serious capital flight to other places, resulting in declining total revenue beyond the short term. In the worst case, the total loss in revenue and employment may more than offset whatever gain that may materialise in Economy II. My reply is that first, the funding of the scheme need not rely heavily on changes in tax structure, given the many alternative options already available. Since the scheme can be looked upon as some kind of public investment bearing a return, it is more plausible to raise funds via bond issue. Second, I do not believe a special tax on the super-rich will stir too much negative reaction. Many super-rich make new investments not because they are keen on maximising return but because they want to keep up with their "investor Joneses". Many of them make investments based more on opportunities available than on how much tax they eventually have to pay as long as they are making money.

Alternatively, instead of taxing a particular group of people (e.g. the super-rich), we can levy tax on some special types of economic activities. What I have in mind in particular is tax from some types of financial activities, especially those that many are not really productive from the viewpoint of the real economy and real production and those that play on highly leveraged mechanisms. A tax on the financial sector to be used exclusively to finance the NPV scheme represents then a transfer of social resources from more speculative activities to the real activities of the less resourceful mass. But as I have pointed out, raising the tax rate should be considered only as the last resort.

There is yet an additional way of achieving a more equitable distribution in society as a whole that can go hand in hand with the NPV scheme, namely the inequality indexation scheme (Shiller, 2012). The idea is to pre-set a scale of overall equity to be attained under a particular time frame and adjust tax rates (either income tax or tax on wealth or both) accordingly. The additional tax revenue so generated which is to be injected into Economy II will then act as an "income leveller". The risk of this joint scheme is that more equity may be attained at the expense of a slower growth for the economy. Thus the scheme, again, should be adopted only as a last resort.

Doubts may arise as to whether the proposed scheme may be option-limiting because some recipients on the conventional dole-out system may fear that their original entitlement may be reduced and the vouchers they receive are of such a restricted nature that they end up worse off than before. This worry, however, can be removed by a smooth transition. The supply side of the scheme can be well nurtured and planned beforehand and the welfare reduction can be delayed until Economy II is in full force. Moreover, qualified voucher recipients if they happen to also be welfare recipients can be given the option of whether they want to stay on the existing dole-out plan or join the voucher scheme. Given the likelihood that the overall value of the vouchers they receive will exceed considerably that of their existing welfare receipt, these welfare recipients should be incentivised to join the new scheme provided that the above-mentioned transition is generally smooth.

As a matter of fact, Economy II is also option-enhancing in terms of the mode of business operation on the part of the employers and the choice of jobs on the part of the employee. Existing small operators that are qualified can choose to switch to the status of natural person company and switch back if they like. If they choose to become natural person companies they will stand to benefit from the buying power of voucher recipients and will face less severe competition. Or they may choose to stick to the original mode of operation, in which case they may face perhaps temporarily a setback in their customer base, some of their old customers being distracted to spending in Economy II. If so, they may be compelled to upgrade the quality of their products or services or to carve out new market niches for survival. On the part of the worker, he can choose to stay within the existing system or he may choose to work in Economy II. To entice more workers to join Economy II, the voucher issuing authority may consider in the initial stage to grant additional subsidy to these workers either in the form of voucher or cash.

To enhance the chance of success, the voucher issuing authority is advised to think through all potential problems that may arise in the process of implementation. Before the launching of the scheme, long-term funding problems, training programmes to be offered and pre-announced marketing and surveillance schemes should be carefully examined. Since the scheme is a semi-closed system with pre-set voucher value by sectors and time frame of implementation, it is relatively easy for the authority to monitor its functioning. To further enhance efficient functioning, the authority can also consider building a macro Economy II-wide information and communications platform so that information flow within Economy II can be made more smooth and transparent.

Another criticism is related to the actual implementation of the scheme. Some voucher recipients may not really need the products or services specified by the vouchers. They may simply dispose of their vouchers on hand to suppliers at a discount, pretending that a genuine transaction had taken place. Both parties thus privately gain through their cheating behaviours, without actually benefiting Economy II. To forestall such abuse, strict rules and high penalties have to be seriously imposed, to be supplemented by vigilant policing and thorough legal enforcement.

There is an important trade-off to consider. To speed up supply in Economy II, firms in Economy I that are qualified (i.e. below certain revenue or profit level or shorter than a specific period of operation) can be encouraged to change their status to operate in Economy II. But the result would be to render Economy II as a playing field less level than it would be than if it were to start from square one. Moreover, some more than qualified existing firms in Economy I, keen on exploiting the big opportunities offered, may first close down their business, apply to form a natural person company and then use the same business resources and structures in their new operation in Economy II. To forestall such malpractice, it may be necessary to set limits on the initial size of Economy II operators, only to relax such limits when Economy II matures.

Another possible difficulty in implementation is in places where a particular factor input is in rigid supply, for example extreme high rental of commercial premises, which can put government in some kind of policy dilemma. Under such circumstances, the government may have to adopt a gradualist approach or to first address the input bottleneck before launching the project.

Over time, we can witness a steady division of labour between the two sectors, with the growth of Economy I largely driven by technological innovation and higher end human capital growth. In periods of technological spurts, the growth of Economy I may outpace that of Economy II by a wide margin, resulting in divergence of average income growth between the two sectors. To address such inequality, it may be useful to link the level of transfer to Economy II to the rate of the growth of Economy I or its tax revenue growth.

One idea of the voucher is to stimulate and to create potential demand for a particular sub-sector, hence attracting potential supplies. If it is considered useful to further stimulate a particular group of suppliers, for example youth entrepreneurs or ethnic groups, the voucher issuing authority may consider giving an extra bonus to these groups by giving the vouchers they earn an additional amount when they are to be exchanged for real money. There is of course a problem of validation, i.e. making sure that the vouchers these group use to exchange for money are actually earned from their economic activities.

Apart from the above, it is likely that we would encounter different unforeseen issues at the level of details and execution, some more general by nature while others are related to specific places and economies. I fear I have to leave them to the voucher issuing authorities, who presumably should be able to learn from mistakes. With well-thought out plans and well-tested efforts, I believe these potential challenges would be effectively addressed.

Notes

1 The idea of dualistic partitioning is not new. The question is how the partitioning is structured. Paul Romer for example, suggested a recipe for growth by way of replicating charter cities and turning them into engines of growth in developing countries. He argued that with better rules and institutions, less developed nations can be set on a more effective trajectory of growth. In his conception, a host country could delegate such an operation to a more developed trustee nation for a specific period

which would nurture new rules of governance. Critics, however, argue that this model has the likely effect of aggravating inequality before the positive impacts can be felt. Some point out that this is merely a copy of classical colonialism. In a sense, the dualist idea is also practised by Deng Xiaoping in his creation of special economic zones and the "one-country-two-system" in Hong Kong.

2   In this book, the term legal person is to be used interchangeably with that of juridical person, although natural persons are, strictly speaking, also legal persons.

3   Basic income guarantee schemes, whether they come in the form of high-sounding names such as "Peoples' Capitalism" by James S. Albus (1976), and however well-intentioned they are, can hardly avoid lapsing into the "culture of dependency" which the NPV model attempts to avoid.

5 Growth Without Inequality

In Part I of this book, I have argued that after a period of relentless growth, the conventional capitalist economy (Economy I) is heading towards a state of weak growth, high debt pile-up and increasing maldistribution. I have also pointed out that this state of affairs is likely to further deteriorate. This is chiefly because the main engines of growth, i.e. the limited liability joint-stock company, the holding company and its counterparts in the financial sector, for example the leverage-promoting bank and other financial institutions, gradually give rise to new "market forms" that unwittingly impoverish the poor and the less resourceful, as well as destabilise the economy through the mispricing of value and risk. In a broad sense, such is the price paid by the present capitalist society for its rapid growth.

What about the future? In Chapter 3 I pointed out that reforming Economy I from within is a gigantic if not almost impossible task, given the enormous economic power wielded by the existing interests coupled with the enfeebled governments that we now witness in most developed nations. This does not mean we should sit back and do nothing. There are a lot of things we can do to "tame" the system. But a truly lasting reform has to dissociate from the existing system and to spring from the outside. This is the logic behind my conception of Economy II, which is to be built outside the existing system and which is to be insulated from the latter's negative influences.

What then are the advantages of this newly created "exogenous" system? What are the ramifications? Briefly put, I believe Economy II, once becoming fully operational, will go a long way in achieving equality, growth and to some extent, enhanced macro-stability for the general economy. In this chapter, I will look at the ramifications of adopting the NPV scheme and the operating outcomes of Economy II from four angles, namely, equality, growth, stability and individual well-being cum social harmony. Before that, I will reiterate briefly the justifications for adopting the scheme.

a   Economy II makes use of the simplest "textbook" "market form", i.e. the free, self-equilibrating and self-regulating market which can be shown to be Pareto-optimal and Pareto-efficient and is supposed to generate the highest level of welfare.

b   Economy II is to be operated solely by the most primitive "corporate forms", i.e. the natural person company and the natural person partnership company. Since Economy II is characterised largely by the provision of mundane needs of everyday life and is designed to suit the relatively less skilled group of society, it is expected to function with a fairly low level of capital goods. With capital playing a small role in Economy II and the natural person eligible to operating only one natural person company, long-term equality can more likely be achieved and assured.

c   Since mass participation is a pre-requisite for economic growth, the vigorous promotion of labour participation and the utilisation of idle human capital in Economy II is conducive to a higher rate of employment and growth than otherwise.

d   Provided that the vouchers are well designed and properly managed, they are in a position to inculcate among the less privileged groups of society a collective vision that the future is investable. A kind of "grassroots capitalism" can thus emerge, leading to a higher rate of human capital formation and subsequent growth at least within Economy II.

e   Since Economy II can now take good care of the least privileged, Economy I is no longer burdened by the need to look after the interest of this mass group. Players in Economy I can now forge ahead full-heartedly without being dragged down by political conflicts over such issues as minimum wage legislation, competition law etc. This may result in a smoother mode of development for Economy I in the longer run.

f   Since Economy II will specialise in labour-intensive and service-intensive industries (especially of the manual kind), a new division of labour and specialisation will take place between it and Economy I in due course. The resulting respective comparative advantages may enhance productivity for the economy as a whole.

In the following, I will look at the merits and advantages of the new dual and compartmentalised economy from four different angles.

5.1 Equality

In the previous chapter, I have dealt at some length with the equitable aspects of Economy II. In the modern mixed economy, the government is supposed to play the role of a referee as well as a provider of a level playing field to ensure that maldistribution in society, especially regarding income, is not getting out of hand. Although governments differ widely in their re-distributive policies and priorities, it is generally recognised that it is the responsibility of the modern civil society to take care of its less privileged members. But as I have laboured to show in the previous chapters, the present-day government finds itself increasingly ill-equipped in discharging this function. Most governments can no doubt take care of the absolutely helpless and the least privileged, hence achieving some kind of minimal equity. However, there is not much it can do in the long run to prevent worsening distributive disparity among the rest of society, particularly as some of its bureaucrats are likely to be captured by the ever-growing power of the super-rich and their formidable predatory corporations. Huge pile-up of debt and servicing cost further tie the hands of the government in maintaining indefinitely a high level of welfare provision. Worse still, some nations in serious fiscal trouble choose to adopt austerity programmes to reduce their burden, resulting in further negative impact on the poor.

In contrast to the kind of "passive equity strategy" or "passive welfarism" practised by governments in the modern mixed economy in the form of handing out welfare dole-outs, whose recipients become attuned to look at these transfer payments as rightful entitlements, the strategy I recommend in the construction of Economy II, albeit containing elements of welfare, is essentially designed to motivate people to earn these benefits.

The equity that will prevail in Economy II is characterised not only by the possibility that participants can be encouraged to earn their benefits (which can be seen as some kind of "active welfarism"), but can also be fine-tuned and adjusted to attain specific economic goals. Besides it is likely to be self-sustainable because we can expect Economy II to generate multiplier effects and grow steadily. Equity is thus achieved not merely by welfare injection, but also through active employment and human capital formation among the less skilful and the less resourceful.

One conventional policy measure to reduce inequality in the mixed economy is to introduce minimum wages. Minimum wage legislation is often considered a necessary evil because it can result in some discrimination against the marginal workers, especially the least skilled group and the young.[1] Even granted that on balance it does more good than harm, minimum wage legislation remains at best a passive policy instrument, for it does nothing to spur the motivation of the workforce. Besides it unavoidably brings about perennial political disputes among the government, employers and employees over the proper level of the minimum. Quite the contrary, voucher injection under the NPV scheme can achieve the same result using the less arbitrary market platform and without causing an equal amount of social tension.

Another set of commonly employed policy measures to achieve some degree of equity are the competition laws and anti-trust laws targeted at attaining fairer competition in the market. While these laws may still be necessary to protect the smaller enterprises in Economy I, they are no longer applicable to the natural person companies in Economy II because by its very design, the NPV scheme provides a highly level playing field for its players. It also provides an exit and a new frontier for those smaller players in Economy I who find it difficult in coping with the intensity or the unfairness of the competition therein.

The kind of equity achievable within Economy II is twofold. The design of the NPV scheme amounts to providing an ideal platform for attaining the goal of equality of opportunity for the less resourceful group in society. This is achievable by providing a conceivably most level playing field for participants with very minimal entry requirement especially in terms of capital, and by sheltering it from the intense and probably unfair competition prevailing in Economy I. As a result, a wide array of both entrepreneurial and employment opportunities open up, especially for those who do not possess much material resources but wish to make a living on their own effort, and those who see work as an important part of their lives but are denied of such opportunity. For the modest person who is not ambitious enough to play the "small" entrepreneurial role by starting a natural person company, the effective subsidy that the vouchers confers (both as a qualified recipient and possibly as a worker for the natural person company) and the ample employment opportunities created in Economy II should enable them to get a decent job and a reasonable wage via the trickle-down effect.

With equality of opportunity thus widely assured and practised, we can expect the second kind of equity, namely "equality of outcome" to be more accessible within Economy II. Note that such "equality of outcome" is not to be achieved by command, nor will it bring about disincentive on the part of the more entrepreneurial members of Economy II or at their expense. By all accounts, the situation is going to be "win-win".

5.2 Growth

It goes almost without saying that we need growth because without it, society would be deprived of "hope" for a large part of its members and is therefore even in danger of fragmentation.[2]

In the aftermath of the 2007–8 financial crisis and already many years on, many governments in the industrial world are still struggling hard to put their economies in order or to put them back to the past trajectories of growth, but with mixed results. Recoveries are pitifully slow, pale and feeble and are often accompanied by joblessness. In our scheme of analysis, this undesirable situation, which is sometimes termed as the "new normal", is something to be expected. Let me highlight a few points.

a   Since conventional monetary policy measures are ineffective especially in a situation where interest rate is at the "zero lower bound", some central banks are compelled to adopt the less conventional method in the form of Quantitative Easing (QE) to stimulate the economy. While the eventual impact of this policy instrument remains to be ascertained, it does not seem to be working as effectively as the conventional one. While the financial sector clearly stands to benefit, the benefit to the real sector remains somewhat elusive and the price to be paid is still unknown.[3]

b   Even after an economy is back to the path of recovery, since growth will continue to empower the super-rich and impoverish the poor over time, aggregate demand would, other things being equal, chronically fall short of aggregate supply, thus dragging down the long-term rate of growth.

c   Chronic unemployment and under-employment result not merely in the destruction of human capital. The social ethos thus generated is not conducive to the perception of the investability of the future, especially among the young. As a matter of fact, the rates of youth unemployment in many places almost double those of general unemployment across the board. The number of young people out of work globally is nearly as big as the population of the US, and at its worst in countries with a rigid labour market characterised by cartelised industries, high taxes on hiring, strict rules on firing and high minimum wages. This staggering long-term destruction of human capital combined with the obstruction of human capital formation will also cap the rate of growth.

d   In the US, the QE presently in force, regardless of its usefulness in stimulating the economy, has been propping up asset prices artificially, meaning that central bankers are stoking inequality, rewarding financial firms despite their past misdeeds and may probably be sowing the seeds of the next crisis. Even if we disregard this potential hazard, we still face the worrying trend that the rich and capital owner are being drawn away from real investment resulting in the continuing mispricing and misallocation of capital. In other words, preservation of wealth and the derivative speculative activities in the financial sector continue to take priority over the creation of wealth though hard and enterprising work in the real sector. Moreover, with "short-termism" prevailing in the business sphere, enterprises have less incentive to make long-term investment and tend to direct more of their effort towards rent-seeking activities. None of these situations is conducive to the healthy growth of the economy.

As an antidote to the sluggishness of the present-day economic situation, Economy II is likely to have a big role to play. For one thing, it will vastly increase the labour participation rate, drawing workforce not only from the unemployed, the under-employed, low-skilled labour and social dropouts, but also from retirees who consider themselves too robust to stop working. This is particularly timely against the backdrop of deteriorating labour participation in some nations, a worldwide trend of ageing and declining demand for low-skilled labour as a result of the increasing employment of robotics and robot technology.[4] With the institution of Economy II, the promise of a new frontier of opportunities with low entry threshold will attract alike the ambitious but small entrepreneurs as well as an "army" of marginalised and potential workforce.

In the course of this mass participation, we can expect a renewal of human capital formation. With new markets emerging through increased demand, we can expect supply to pour in from different quarters to exploit the opportunities presented. As supply responds to the new level of demand, formation of human capital of different descriptions will take place. A vibrant spirit of "grassroots capitalism" will soon replace the general pessimism in today's slow-moving economies.

behind is singularly the elimination of under-performers. It is, therefore, not surprising that its supporting education system is elite-oriented, picking the "best performers" by standards based on a curriculum guided by the frontiers of knowledge and technology and geared to state-of-the-art industrial production and professional services. By corollary, its examination system acts in effect as a screening and selection mechanism to meet the high quality manpower needs of big corporations and professional organisations.

As a result of the above development, two closely related consequences follow. The first is a disproportionately high reward to the best performers, especially those possessing innovative capabilities and the second, a rat-race competition and its throat-cutting social ethos. Needless to say, the mechanisms in question serve pretty well the goal of economic growth especially in the short and the medium term.

Such growth, however, is not achieved without a cost. The economic cost of maldistribution as well as its long-term subversive effect on growth itself has already been dealt with in detail in this book. The social cost is also fully dealt with in the standard literatures of sociology and politics and barely needs to be further elaborated here. Suffice it to say that the steeper the social pyramid becomes in terms of income, wealth and opportunities, the more precarious are the participants and the more plentiful are the potential dropouts. Worse still, an unintended consequence of an elite-driven economy leading to a quickening pace of technological progress is that it renders the rest of the members increasingly marginal and irrelevant. The rest of the familiar story is the deteriorating level of unemployment and real wage stagnation.

There is, therefore, no exaggeration to say that the material well-being and prosperity of the modern "mono-excellence" society is achieved at no small cost. At the societal level, it is achieved at the expense of an increasingly large number of real or disguised dropouts. At the level of the individual, it is attained through paying the intangible but real psychological cost manifest in tension, anxiety, fear of loss, sense of inferiority etc. of the individual, all conveniently swept under the carpet by the abstract notion of the economic man.

All these will undergo drastic changes with the advent of Economy II which addresses the fundamental plight of the low-skilled, the less resourceful mass in society. By barring competition from Economy I and the aggression of its rent-capturing elites and by creating a self-contained system paying a reasonable premium on labour and low skilled activities, Economy II takes on the role of a social safety valve in the most comprehensive manner. Even as it encourages competition within its own sphere, it takes away the intense pressure and tension inherent in the existing capitalist regime.

Importantly, the low achievers and the low-performing students in the education system now need not face the dire consequences of failure in the rat-race competition. A wide array of options is now open to them in Economy II. Most of these do not require high academic attainment. Indeed, Economy II can readily be designed to accommodate multi-talents and multi-skills. Economy II, in short, can be made to target at multiple excellences and to encourage the thriving of a diversity of skills albeit not belonging necessarily to the Hi-tech type. One may question whether the relaxation of the said competition may slow down the overall rate of human capital formation essential to driving the capitalist economy. This is of course anybody's guess. But considering that growth is a phenomenon of mass activity, Economy II, by inducing mass participation in entrepreneurship and hence capital formation, is not necessarily worse off than the present system, which is characterised by high-performing elites alongside a huge number of dropouts and disguised dropouts. Moreover, mature entrepreneurs developed within Economy II may decide to join and have spill-over effects on Economy I in driving growth in the later rounds of development.

Immersed in the newly evolved individuated order of humanity, the more enlightened among us are naturally inclined to celebrate the supremacy of the individual and to take him to be the source and centre of all social values. This, in essence, is the gist of modern liberalism, thought to be achievable if we have full constitutional and legal protection of individual rights and liberties as well as a free market granting the individual opportunities to realise his full potential.

Let me for the time refrain from debating whether or not such an arrangement is the most suitable for the long-term good of humankind and accept provisionally this doctrine in good faith.[6] The question is whether or not the free market as practised in Economy I is a good enough platform. And as I have shown in this book, the answer is a qualified yes because while a free market does provide a valuable venue for innovation, creativity and growth, the unintended long-term effect is that growing corporations directed by a small circle of elites and their "accomplices" manage to capture the bulk of the benefits, leaving scant resources for the rest to explore their potentials. Self-realisation, supposedly a dream for all, is thus restricted in practice to only a relatively small section of the population. Modern liberalism, in pursuit of the ideal of unleashing the potential of each individual for self-realisation, is quietly subverted as capitalism progresses into maturity.

But with the advent of Economy II, which can be designed to make room for multiple skills, self-realisation of personal potential for a large section of the population on a long-term basis is now possible. Equality of opportunity, a necessary condition for the self-realisation of individual members of society, is now amply provided for in Economy II. In short, Economy II is the truly needed and workable platform upon which the ideal of individualism is to be achieved.[7]

Partly as a result of the promotion of self-actualisation and the well-being of the individual, Economy II also contributes to social harmony in the following manner.

a   By providing extensive employment opportunities among those keen on work, Economy II confers on a larger section of people a sense of social participation on top of the chance for self-realisation. Such a sense of social participation, i.e. the feeling that one can make a useful contribution to society together with others via work, naturally enhances social cohesion.

b   It helps reduce political tension in society. This is because it is no longer necessary for the bulk of the citizens to engage in an incessant and even escalating struggle against the super-rich and their agents, hence removing much room for manipulative activities by the politician. Political parties will also lose part of their appeal as the economic well-being of the mass improves and stabilises.

c   Social tension, apart from being caused by maldistribution, is often caused by the special interests and values of different ethnic groups in a society. While Economy I is hardly competent in removing the political and ideological elements that accompany these ethnic conflicts, a much more even income distribution resulting from the operation of Economy II can go a long way to alleviating such tensions, which often originate from and are reinforced by economic factors. In many places, minority ethnic groups are, almost as a rule, economically less resourceful. The specific vouchers in Economy II can be tailored to benefit specifically these groups, thus helping to reduce the intensity of such tension.

d   As I have pointed out in the last section, Economy II unwittingly promotes the local economy and confers big benefits on the local community. As we all know, a prospering local community is an important pillar for building harmony in any society, as the communitarian strongly believes.

By taking pressure out of the present-day rat-race education system, by enabling individuals to pursue their different interests and develop their different talents, by fostering social and ethnic harmony and so on, Economy II is more than an economic system. It is a system that provides for equality of opportunity in the true sense, one that unleashes the potential of the individual, one that raises the dignity of those who are less academically gifted, one that gives more psychological comfort and peace to the less competitive, one that provides a more stable work environment and more predictable return for most people, and one that can promise a harmonious and prosperous local community. In short, the function of Economy II goes beyond the building of a stable and growing economy. It provides the very recipe to build a happier society, populated by happier individuals.

Notes

1   Note however, that studies over different places and time show that the effects of minimum wage legislation can differ widely, and can result in few negative impacts in certain situations and cases.
2   This insight goes far back to Adam Smith.
3   In benefitting the financial sector and thus the moneyed class, it is likely to have negative effect on wealth distribution to the disadvantage of the mass.

4 Japan, for instance, has over a quarter of a million robots.
5 Chapter 2 of this book gives an analysis of the sources of instability of the financial sector, namely, the excess credit growth made possible by leveraged mechanisms weakening the budget constraint of investors, the lack of a two dimensional reality check mechanism for appraising the value of financial products unlike in the case of the goods market and the cognitive asymmetry between Risk I and Risk II. Since economic cycles of today's economies are largely financial in nature, the above factors apply to the economic system as a whole.
6 I will deal with this issue in my new work "Progress without Injustice: Reinventing Politics".
7 Amartya Sen looks at income inequality and poverty as the result of "capability deprivation". His ideal is to widen people's choices and the level of their achieved well-being through increasing functionings, capabilities and agency (1999). This is best achieved via the platform of Economy II.

Further Reading

Abramovitz, M. (1993) "The Search for the Sources of Growth: Areas of Ignorance, Old and New", *Journal of Economic History*, 53.2, 217–243

Acemoglu, D. and J. A. Robinson, (2012) *Why Nations Fail: The Origins of Power, Prosperity and Poverty*, London: Allen Lane

Adler, M. (2010) *Economics for the Rest of Us: Debunking the Science That Makes Life Dismal*, New York: The New Press

Admati, A. and M. Hellwig (2013) *The Bankers' New Clothes: What's Wrong with Banking and What to Do About It*, Princeton: Princeton University Press

Aghion, P. and P. Howitt. (1992) "A Model of Growth through Creative Destruction", *Econometrica*, 60, 323–351

Aghion, P. and P. Howitt (2009) *The Economics of Growth*, Cambridge, Mass.: MIT

Akerlof, G. A. and R. J. Schiller (2009) *Animal Spirits: How Human Psychology Drives the Economy, and Why It Matters for Global Capitalism*, Princeton: Princeton University Press

Albus, J. S. (1976) *Peoples' Capitalism: The Economics of the Robot Revolution*, College Park: Md.: New World Books

Arrow, K. J. (1962) "The Economic Implications of Learning by Doing", *Review of Economic Studies*, 29, 155–173

Arrow, K. J. and F. H. Hahn (1954) "Existence of an Equilibrium in Economics for a Competitive Economy", *Econometrica*, 22, 265–290

Arrow, K. J. and F. H. Hahn (1971) *General Competitive Analysis*, San Francisco: Holden-Day

Arthur, B. (1994) *Increasing Returns and Path Dependence in the Economy*, Ann Arbor: The University of Michigan Press

Atkinson, A. (2014) *Inequality: What Can Be Done?*, Cambridge, Mass.: Harvard University Press

Bernanke, R. S. (2013) *The Federal Reserve and the Financial Crisis*, Princeton: Princeton University Press

Blinder, A. S. (2013) *After the Music Stopped: The Financial Crisis, the Response, and the Work Ahead*, New York: The Penguin Press

Block, Walter (1996) "Hayek's Road to Serfdom". *Journal of Libertarian Studies*, 12(2), 339–365

Boyer, R. and A. Orlean (1992) "How do Conventions Evolve?", *Journal of Evolutionary Economics*, 2, 165–177

Brummer, A. (2008) *The Crunch: How Greed and Incompetence Sparked the Credit Crisis*, London: Random House Business Books

Buchanan, J. M. and G. Tullock (1962) *The Calculus of Consent: Logical Foundations of Constitutional Democracy*, Ann Arbor: University of Michigan Press

Chang, H. J. (2011) *23 Things They Don't Tell You About Capitalism*, London: Penguin Books

Coase, R. H. (1937) "The Nature of the Firm", *Economica*, 2(1), 133–163

Coggan, P. (2011) *Paper Promises: Money, Debt and the New World Order*, London: Penguin Books

Commons, J. R. (1934) *Institutional Economics*, New York: Macmillan

Conard, E. (2012) *Unintended Consequences: Why Everything You've Been Told About the Economy Is Wrong*, New York: Portfolio Penguin

Cooper, G. (2008) *The Origin of Financial Crises*, New York: Vintage Books

Cowen, T. (2011) *The Great Stagnation*, London: Penguin Books

Coyle, D. (2007) *The Soulful Science: What Economists Really Do and Why It Matters*, Princeton: Princeton University Press

Crouch, C. (2013) *Making Capitalism Fit for Society*, Cambridge: Polity Press

Davidson, P. (2005) *The Keynes Solution: The Path to Global Economic Prosperity*, New York: Palgrave Macmillan

Drucker, P. (1964) *Managing for Result*, New York: Harper & Row

Ferguson, N. (2009) *The Ascent of Money: A Financial History of the World*, London: Penguin Books

Ferguson, N. (2012) *The Great Degeneration: How Institutions Decay and Economies Die*, London: Allen Lane

Foroohar, R. (2016) *Makers and Takers*, New York: Crown Business

Frank, R. H. (2011) *The Darwin Economy: Liberty, Competition and the Common Good*, Princeton: Princeton University Press

Friedman, M. (1953) *Essays in Positive Economics*, Chicago: University of Chicago Press

Friedman, M. (1968) "The Role of Monetary Policy", *American Economic Review*, 58(1), 1–17

Galbraith, J. K. (1958) *The Affluent Society*, Boston: Houghton Mifflin

Galbraith, J. K. (1967) *The New Industrial State*, Boston: Houghton Mifflin

Galbraith, James K. (2014) *The End of Normal: The Great Crisis and the Future of Growth*, New York: Simon & Schuster

Galor, Oded (2011) *Unified Growth Theory*, Princeton: Princeton University Press

Gray, J. (1998) *False Dawn: The Delusions of Global Capitalism*, London: Granta Publications

Greenepan, A. (2013) *The Map and the Territory 2.0: Risk, Human Nature and the Future of Forecasting*, London: Penguin Books

Hahn, F. H. (1973) *On the Notion of Equilibrium in Economics: An Inaugural Lecture*, Cambridge: Cambridge University Press

Harrod, R. F. (1939) "An Essay in Dynamic Theory", *Economic Journal*, 49, 14–33

Hayek, F. A. (1944) *The Road to Serfdorm*, London: Routledge & Kegan Paul

Hayek, F. A. (1967) *Studies in Philosophy, Politics and Economics*, London: Routledge & Kegan Paul

Hayek, F. A. (1978) *New Studies in Philosophy Politics, Economics and the History of Ideas*, London: Routledge & Kegan Paul

Henry, P. B. (2013) *Turnaround: Third World Lessons for First World Growth*, New York: Basic Books

Heuvel, K. V. (2009) *Meltdown: How Greed and Corruption Shattered Our Financial System and How We Can Recover*, New York: Nation Books

Hollingsworth, R. and R. Boyerl (eds) (1997) *Contemporary Capitalism: The Embeddedness of Institutions*, Cambridge, Mass.: Cambridge University Press

Jarsulic, M. (2010) *Anatomy of a Financial Crisis: A Real Estate Bubble, Runaway Credit Markets and Regulatory Failure*, New York: Palgrave Macmillan

Kahneman, D. (2011) *Thinking, Fast and Slow*, London: Penguin Books

King, S. D. (2010) *Losing Control: The Emerging Threats to Western Prosperity*, New Haven & London: Yale University Press

King, S. D. (2013) *When the Money Runs Out: The End of Western Affluence*, New Haven & London: Yale University Press

Kaldor, N. (1957) "A Model of Economic Growth", *The Economic Journal*, 67(268), 591–624

Kotler, P. (2015) *Confronting Capitalism: Real Solution for a Troubled Economic System*, New York: Amacon

Kroszner, R. S. and R. J. Shiller (2011) *Reforming U.S. Financial Markets: Reflections Before and Beyond Dodd-Frank*, Cambridge, Mass.: MIT

Krugman, P. (2013) *End This Depression Now*, New York and London: W.W. Norton & Company

Kutznets, S. (1955) "Economic Growth and Income Equality", *American Economic Review*, 45(1), 1–28

Lucas, R. E. (1972) "Expectation and the Neutrality of Money", *Journal of Economic Theory*, 4(2), 103–124

Lucas, R. E. (1988) "On the Mechanics of Economic Development", *Journal of Monetary Economics*, 22, 3–42

Madrick, J. (2014) *Seven Bad Ideas: How Mainstream Economists Have Damaged America and the World*, New York: Random House

Mason, P. (2015) *PostCapitalism: A Guide to Our Future*, London: Allen Lane

Mauldin, J. and J. Tepper (2011) *Endgame: The End of the Debt Supercycle and How it Changes Everything*, Hoboken, NJ: John Wiley and Sons

Mian, A. and A. Sufi (2014) *House of Debt: How They (and You) Carried the Great Recession, and How We Can Prevent It from Happening Again*, Chicago: The University of Chicago Press

Minsky, H. P. (1982) *Can "It" Happen Again? Essays on Instability and Finance*, Armonk, NY: M. F. Sharpe

Minsky, H. P. (2008) *Stabilizing an Unstable Economy*, New York: McGraw-Hill

Morgenson, G. and J. Rosner (2011) *Reckless Endangerment: How Outsized Ambition, Greed, and Corruption Created the Worst Financial Crisis of Our Time*, New York: Time Books/St. Martin's Griffin

Moyo, D. (2012) *How the West was Lost*, London: Penguin Books

North, D. C. (1990) *Institutions, Institutional Change and Economic Performance*, Cambridge and New York: Cambridge University Press

Nozick, R. (1974) *Anarchy, State, and Utopia*, New York: Basic Books

Patel, R. (2009) *The Value of Nothing: How to Reshape Market Society and Redefine Democracy*, New York: Picador

Phelps, E. (2013) *Mass Flourishing: How Grassroots Innovation Created Jobs, Challenges and Change*, Princeton: Princeton University Press

Philip, K. (2008) *Bad Money: Reckless Finance, Failed Politics, and the Global Crisis of American Capitalism*, London: Penguin Books

Piketty, T. (2014) *Capital in the Twenty-First Century*, Cambridge, Mass.: Belknap Press

Polanyi, K. (1946) *The Great Transformation*, New York: Rinehart

Poole, E. (2015) *Capitalism's Toxic Assumptions: Redefining Next Generation Economics*, London: Bloomsbury

Rajan, R. G. (2010) *Fault Lines: How Hidden Fractures Still Threaten the World Economy*, Princeton and Oxford: Princeton University Press

Reich, R. B. (2011) *AfterShock: The Next Economy and America's Future*, New York: Vintage Books

Reinhart, C. and K. Rogoff (2009) *This Time Is Different: Eight Centuries of Financial Folly*, Princeton: Princeton University Press

Richards, J. (2014) *The Death of Money: The Coming Collapse of the International Monetary System*, London: Portfolio Penguin

Rodrik, D. (2007) *One Economics Many Recipes: Globalization, Institutions and Economic Growth*, Princeton: Princeton University Press

Romer, P. (1990) "Endogenous Technological Change", *Journal of Political Economy*, 98(5): 71–102

Rostow, W. W. (1959) *The Stages of Economic Growth: A Non-Communist Manifesto*, Cambridge: Cambridge University Press

Rotler, P. (2015) *Confronting Capitalism: Real Solutions for a Troubled Economic System*, New York: Amacon

Roubini, N. and S. Mikm (2010) *Crisis Economics*, London: Penguin

Sachs, J. (2012) *The Price of Civilization: Reawakening Virtue and Prosperity After the Economic Fall*, London: Vintage Books

Schlefer, J. (2012) *The Assumptions Economists Make*, Cambridge, Mass. and London: Belknap Press of Harvard University Press

Sen, A. (1999) *Development as Freedom*, New York: Anchor Books

Sheng, A. (2012) "Is the Chinese Growth Model Replicable?" In O. Blanchard, D. Romer, M. Spence and J. Stiglitz (eds) *The Wake of the Crisis*, Cambridge, Mass. and London: MIT Press

Shiller, R. J. (2000) *Irrational Exuberance*, Princeton: Princeton University Press

Shiller, R. J. (2012) *Finance and the Good Society*, Princeton and Oxford: Princeton University Press

Skene, L. and M. Kidd (2013) *Surviving the Debt Storm: Getting Capitalism Back on Track*, London: Profile Books

Smithers, A. (2013) *The Road to Recovery: How and Why Economic Policy Must Change*, Chichester: John Wiley & Sons Ltd

Solow, R. M. (1956) "A Contribution to the Theory of Economic Growth", *Quarterly Journal of Economics*, 70, 65–94

Solow, R. (1957) "Technical Change and the Aggregate Production Function", *Review of Econometrics and Statistics*, 43, 217–235

Soros, G. and G. P. Schmitz (2014) *The Tragedy of the European Union: Disintegration or Revival?* New York: Public Affairs

Stiglitz, J. E. (2010) *Freefall: America, Free Markets, and the Shrinking of the World Economy*, New York and London: W. W. Norton & Company

Stiglitz, J. E. (2012) *The Price of Inequality: How Today's Divided Society Endangers Our Future*, New York: W.W. Norton & Company

Turner, A. (2012) *Economics After the Crisis: Objectives and Means*, Cambridge, Mass.: The MIT Press

Tversky, A. and D. Kahneman (1981) "The Framing of Decisions and the Psychology of Choice", *Science*, 211, 453–458

Varoufakis, Y. (2011) *The Global Minotaur*, London: Zed Books

Veblen, T. (1898) "Why is Economics Not an Evolutionary Science", *The Quarterly Journal of Economics*, 12(4), 373–397

Wallerstein, I., R. Collins, M. Mann, G. Derluguian and C. Calhoun (2013) *Does Capitalism Have a Future?*, Oxford: Oxford University Press

Weiner, E. J. (2010) *The Shadow Market*, New York:Scribner

Williamson, O. (1985) *The Economic Institutions of Capitalism*, New York: The Free Press

Woo, H. K. H. (1992) *Cognition, Value and Price*, Ann Arbor: Michigan University Press

Woo, H. K. H. (1997) *The Reign of the Legal Person*, Hong Kong: University of Hong Kong Press

Index

For Product Safety Concerns and Information please contact our EU
representative GPSR@taylorandfrancis.com
Taylor & Francis Verlag GmbH, Kaufingerstraße 24, 80331 München, Germany